P9-BXV-230

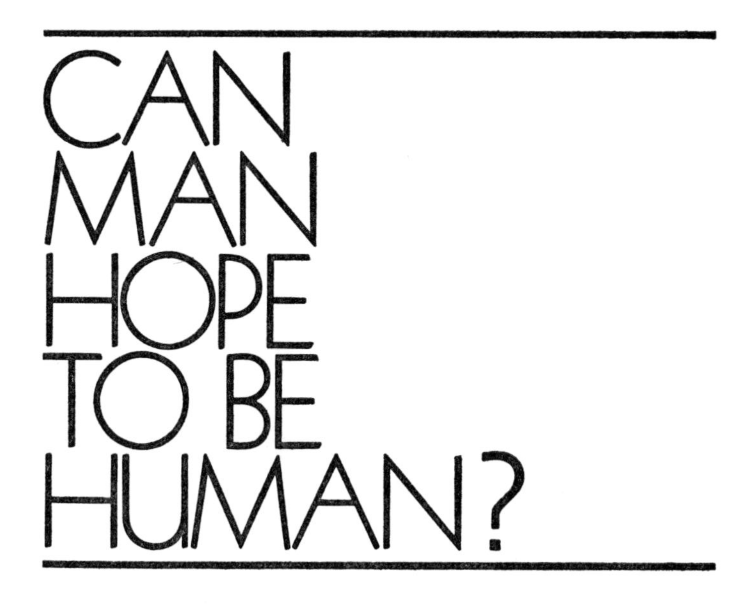
CAN
MAN
HOPE
TO BE
HUMAN?

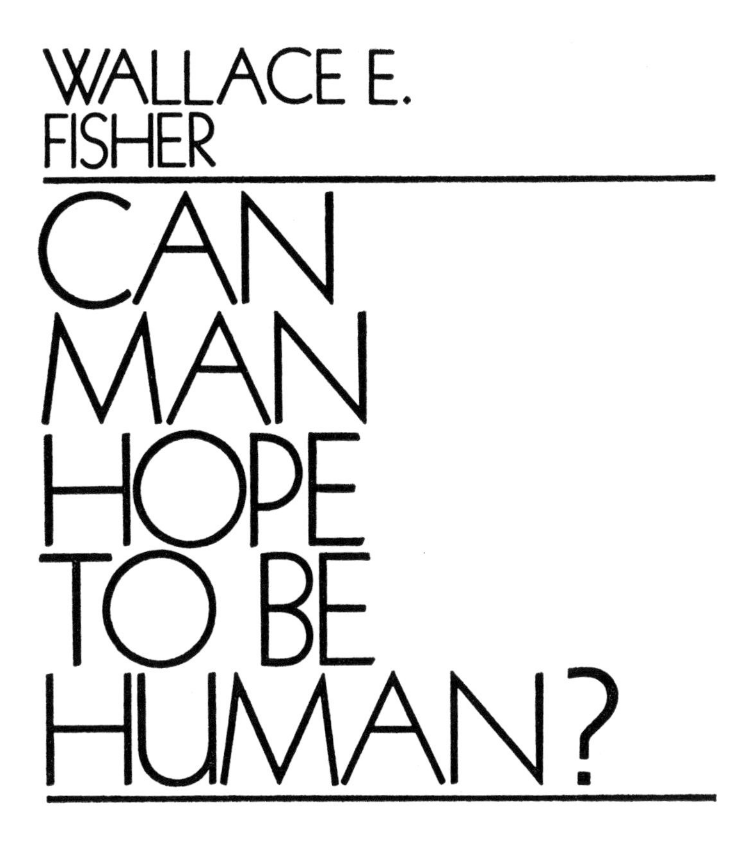
WALLACE E.
FISHER
CAN
MAN
HOPE
TO BE
HUMAN?

ABINGDON PRESS NASHVILLE AND NEW YORK

CAN MAN HOPE TO BE HUMAN?



*ISBN 0-687-04613-0*

*Library of Congress Catalog Card Number: 75-138276*



SET UP, PRINTED, AND BOUND BY THE PARTHENON PRESS, AT NASHVILLE, TENNESSEE, UNITED STATES OF AMERICA

*To the generation of youth*
*whose brief encounter with*
*the grandeur and misery of man*
*offers a hint that they may alter much*
*that has discouraged and defeated*
*the generation which gave them life—*
*and opportunity*

# PREFACE

Can man hope to be human in a society which militates against his best efforts to be? Can man hope to be human in a society which spawns forces which dehumanize him? Can man hope to be human in a society which loosens the demoniac in him? The churches first raised these questions, but only theoretically. It was the racial minorities and the youth who took the questions existentially to America's streets and campuses. Then segments of "middle America"—stirred by Cambodia, the tragedies at Kent State and Jackson State, abusive rhetoric against the young, bureaucratic government, and inflation—began recognizing the urgent relevance of the questions in their own lives.

During the 1960's the institutional church was prodded to get where the action is. "The church in the world" became the primary issue in ecclesiastical circles. Unfortunately, too many churchmen discovered that if they "talked up" this issue they could insulate the institutional church and themselves against the radical demands of renewal in the biblical sense. Consequently, the 1970's dawned with a church polarized between clergy and laity, between renewalists and status-quoers, and between secularists and spiritualists. The prospects for resolving this cleavage without fundamental changes in the religious establishments and their comfortable constituencies are not sanguine. Certainly the deepening cleavage will not be resolved in favor of "the church in the world" until "the world in the church" is persuaded to accept the Lordship of Christ in its daily life. The church cannot capture the loyalty, or even the interest, of blacks, Mexican-Americans, Puerto Ricans, Indians, teen-agers, young marrieds, or competent middle-agers until its members learn to "listen with affection" to the majority outside the church *and* to join with concerned people from all strata in the world community in the quest for peace, human dignity, and meaning.

The material presented here incorporates insights gained from listening to the world, judgments formed in association with "concerned" people of all persuasions, points of view structured in living uneasily in the institutional church, and convictions shaped by the gospel. It is cast in plain words, because what one sees clearly and believes critically can be stated simply. This is not to suggest, however, a simplistic Faith. The contrary is the case: commitment to Christ complicates human experience. We are seeking here to remember that the New Testament used the language of the homes, shops, political arena, and trade routes (koine Greek).

This material has benefitted from critical exposure at Trinity Church, Lancaster, and from give-and-take associations in several denominational and interdenominational gatherings: a United Church of Christ, Central Pennsylvania, Lenten Retreat; a Methodist Pastors' Annual Conference, Alabama-Florida; the Fifty-first Ohio Pastors' Convocation; the Twenty-ninth Pastors' Institute at Princeton Theological Seminary; the Eighth Annual Convention of the Central Pennsylvania Synod, Lutheran Church in America; the Lutheran Theological Seminary at Columbus, American Lutheran Church;

a Methodist Pastors' Conference of the Dakotas; and a half dozen college campuses. It is presented as

- a series of critical essays for searching individuals—young, middle-aged, and older;
- a study book for discussion groups in the parish, on the campus, and in military circles; and as
- resource material for parish pastors, chaplains, lay teachers, and parents.

Several friends in the professional ministry—Jack R. Hoffman and Vincent R. Eshelman (associates at Trinity); R. Ray Evelan, Harrisburg, Pennsylvania, and Larry L. Lehman, Altoona, Pennsylvania (former associates at Trinity); Gabriel Fackre, Boston, Massachusetts; Harald S. Sigmar, Tacoma, Washington; and William R. Snyder, Minneapolis, Minnesota—read the manuscript and made helpful comments. Wilfred P. Bennett, engineer, RCA; Mrs. Ruth Grigg Horting, former Secretary of Welfare in Pennsylvania; David King and Harry Lane, professors of biology, Franklin and Marshall College; Mrs. Ann Haagen Musselman, high school teacher; Ann Bolbach White, Ph.D.; Robert W. Witmer, M.D., assistant professor of surgery, the University of Pennsylvania School of Medicine; and Susan Zimmerman, college student, offered technical suggestions which clarified the presentation. My secretary, Mrs. Arline S. Fellenbaum, patiently typed several drafts of the manuscript as the material was clarified by encounters in the field. Finally, my wife, Margaret Elizabeth, and our son, Mark, contributed ideas and insights which are incorporated throughout the book. My debt to both on all counts outruns any formal expression of gratitude.

*Wallace E. Fisher*

# CONTENTS

*The last temptation is the greatest treason;*
*to do the right deed for the wrong reason.*
—T. S. Eliot

# I

# CAN MAN HOPE TO BE HUMAN?

Can man hope to be human in a society which militates against his best efforts to be? Can man hope to be human in a society which spawns forces which dehumanize him? Can man hope to be human in a society which loosens the demoniac in him? The churches first raised these questions, but only theoretically. It was the racial minorities and the youth who asked the questions existentially on America's streets and campuses. Now, segments of "middle America"—stirred by Cambodia, the tragedies at Kent State and Jackson State, the abusive rhetoric against the young, an unresponsive government, and inflation—are also asking these questions existentially.

The bubbling optimism that surged across Western society in the nineteenth century and in the early years of this century has evaporated. Unexpectedly, America too has lost her buoyant spirit. A pervasive pessimism, with deepening pockets of cynicism, has settled into the marrow of Western man's bones. Except for an exciting minority, his young are also infected. To some, the wave of the future appears to favor neither East nor West but "the Third World." The democratic West where men probe psyches, transplant human organs, and journey to the moon must employ coercion, scarcely less than the Communist East, to keep national constituencies and political satellites "loyal" to their traditions and goals.

In today's boiling cauldron of social change, what can man expect of himself? The question is crucial, for his expectations affect his attitude toward political action, education, economic planning, sex—the whole range of human life.

> The political, social, and economic structure of a society is largely determined by its answer to this vital question ("What is man?"). Is man a person or a pawn? Is he a cog in the wheel of the state or a free, creative being capable of accepting responsibility. This inquiry is as old as ancient man and as new as the morning newspaper.[1]

Presently, many Americans, especially those under thirty, question whether contemporary social and political institutions can be altered sufficiently to serve human needs effectively. But too few, at any age, inquire seriously whether *man-as-he-is* can recast his institutions to serve persons and thereafter administer them responsibly. Should one seek to be a "responsible self" in an urban-technological society? Should one opt "to do his thing" while society goes to pieces? Should one, "nauseated" by life's dehumanizing demands, react negatively against everything?

There is general agreement that man must pull himself together if he wants to keep his world from being blown to pieces by nuclear missiles, fragmented by disruptive minorities, shattered into atomistic social units by distrust between the generations and the sexes and the races, or smothered by poverty, population, and pollu-

[1] Martin Luther King, Jr., *The Strength to Love* (New York: Harper, 1963), p. 87.

tion. Man can now produce long-range missiles more readily than he can establish justice and order among revolutionary forces in Africa and Asia and Latin America. He can transplant human hearts more successfully than he can reunify Germany or end the imperialistic war in Vietnam. He can expand the national economy more consistently than he can extend the frontiers of racial brotherhood—even in "the land of the free." Obviously, the human equation is not less significant in the building of the good society than the structural-institutional equation. Human problems are always social in scope, but they are never *simply* social. Without "responsible selves" to administer them, flexible institutional structures are socially irrelevant.

> In the last two decades or so the world has seen, in rapid and almost bewildering sequence, convincing and cumulative evidence of the advance in man's control over his natural environment. . . . This yawning and ever-widening gap between human effectiveness in the physical sciences and the puniness of human achievement in the socio-political arena threatens the world with an alternative of catastrophes: annihilation on the one hand; or, on the other, the survival of islands of opulent frustration amidst starvation.[2]

Recognizing that the human equation is primary, the biblical view of man contends that there is a structural fault in his nature which only God can cope with. The classical views of man, still influential in Western society, do not reflect the biblical view. The rationalist denies that there is a structural weakness in man. The naturalist insists that "the leopard cannot change his

[2] The foreword by Thomas Balogh in Rene Cumont and Bernard Rosier, *The Hungry Future,* trans. Rosamund Linnell and R. B. Sutcliffe, (New York: Praeger, 1969).

spots." The existentialist argues that the leopard should not try to change his spots. This widespread confusion is part of the human equation. The biblical view recognizes that man has always been his own most vexing problem. Instinctively, man knows that he is ambivalent. Sensitive people confess daily to one another: "Forgive me; I'm not myself today!" They inquire of themselves, "Why did I behave *that* way?" Human nature is ambiguous, unpredictable. Loren Eiseley, Benjamin Franklin Professor of Anthropology at the University of Pennsylvania, puts it this way: "Man is not completed—that is the secret of his paradoxical behavior. He is not made. He is, perhaps, about to be. Once long ago in the Middle Ages he was called *Homo duplex*—a thing half of dust and half of spirit. The term well expresses his predicament." [3]

It is in man's nature to despoil his true humanity. He rolls in the mud, sticks his nose in his neighbor's business, casts an envious eye on what belongs to another, uses power for his own ends, burns his cities, pollutes his air, and ravages his own and others' countrysides. That is the nature of the human critter. But is that view of itself a balanced representation of man? There are also occasions when he demonstrates an amazing concern for others: he takes a heroic position, expresses honest concern for others, gives beyond his means, and lays down his life for his friend or for his principles. He criticizes his young unmercifully, yet he educates them. He invents and uses atomic and napalm bombs while working simultaneously for a stable international order. Pascal provides the classic description of this

[3] "An Evolutionist Looks at Modern Man," *Adventures of the Mind* (First Series), Richard Thruelsen and John Kohler, eds. (New York: Alfred A. Knopf, 1961), p. 14. See also Loren Eiseley, *The Immense Journey* (New York: Random House, 1957) for his scientific and pragmatic insights into the nature of man.

schizoid fault in man: "What a chimera then is man, what a novelty, what a monster, what chaos, what a subject of contradiction, what a prodigy! Judge of all things, yet an imbecile earthworm; depository of truth, yet a sewer of uncertainty and error; pride and refuse of the universe." [4]

Human life is a mosaic of failure and achievement, frustration and satisfaction, misery and grandeur. No man can be certain what he will *be* in any particular moment or what he will *do* in any concrete situation. This innate disorientation is further complicated by the social dynamics set in motion by other equally disoriented selves. H. Richard Niebuhr frames this reality perceptively:

> I see my human condition, my condition in self-hood rather, and that of my companions, as one of internal division and conflict because though I am one and though they are one in themselves, yet I and they are surrounded by many agencies, many systems of actions upon the self; these are diverse from each other, and to their actions the self makes unreconciled, ununified responses. . . . But the agencies that act upon me remain manifold and so I am manifold. I am I; I am one; yet I lack the actual integrity that is demanded by, or implicit in, my existence as a self.
>
> I have too many selves to know the one.
> In too complex a schooling was I bred,
> Child of too many cities who have gone
> Down all bright cross-roads of the world's desires,
> And at too many altars bowed my head
> To light too many fires.
>
> I become more deeply involved in conflict within myself and in my world when I protest against this inner manifoldness by turning from the many systems of action upon me to myself. . . .

[4] Blaise Pascal, *Pensées*, Louis Lafuma ed., John Warrington, tr. (New York: E. P. Dutton, 1961), p. 65.

This state of sin, or of wretchedness and lostness, seems like the state to which the New Testament writers refer when they speak of man's subjection to principalities and powers and the rulers of the darkness of this world.[5]

Modern man, unlike the Psalmist, does not inquire of God, "What is man that thou art mindful of him?" He does not know God well enough to be that intimate. But modern man does brood over his ambiguous nature, his unpredictable destiny, the meaning of his life. He yearns to know whether he is made for grandeur or misery. Is he hero or coward, creator or destroyer, saint or sinner—or a mysterious mixture of both? Lincoln was not righteous; Stanton was not a devil. Francis of Assisi was not an untainted saint; Atilla the Hun was not a total monster. Gary Cooper's sheriff in "High Noon" was not pure hero; Dustin Hoffman's anti-hero in "The Graduate" had his moments of dogged heroism. And what, some ask, of that *man*, Jesus? Does his authentic person mock mortal man or is he the reason man can hope to become truly human too? Gregory Baum, Catholic theologian, puts this hope in language that modern man understands.

The ambiguity in human life is universal. There is no island of holiness which is totally separated from sin. Jesus refused to divide mankind into just and sinners. In fact, the division of men into categories such as just and sinner, healthy and sick, redeemed and unredeemed, rational and irrational is contrary to reality, and it is the source of suffering and exploitation. If a group of people call themselves just (or healthy) and look upon others as sinners (or sick), they create conditions in which these others will fall more deeply into their plight. The people who call themselves

[5] *The Responsible Self* (New York: Harper & Row, 1963), pp. 137-38. The poem quoted is "A Plaint of Complexity" by Eunice Tietjens, from *Body and Raiment* (New York: Alfred A. Knopf, 1919).

just (or healthy), moreover, will have to live up to their self-created image; they will refuse to come to self-knowledge and, by not looking at who they really are, they, too, will fall more deeply into the plight from which they wish to be freed. Any attempt to understand mankind as an island of the saved surrounded by an ocean of sin destroys life.

For the sake of escaping the powers that keep men from growing up and becoming more human the universal ambiguity of life must be acknowledged.[6]

The idealistic interpretation of man which exalts his rational faculties actually over-estimates human potential. Events in this century have demonstrated that man's rationality is not dependable: the Nazi's coldly calculated extermination of six million Jews, the Communist blood purges in Russia and China, the mushroom cloud over Hiroshima, the nuclear arms race, the smouldering racism in the United States and South Africa. Sociopolitical-technological events have badly shaken, perhaps shattered, Western man's arrogant confidence in his rational faculties. It is because he has been so irrational (bigotry, poverty, war) that a rising tide of sensitive people, having expected something better of man, have turned their backs on both Christianity and humanism during this century.

Man often does the evil which his reason rejects. Mark Antony was willing to let Rome sink in the Tiber as long as he could wile away his days with Cleopatra. The Renaissance popes preferred to let the world into the church rather than to lead the church into the world. The metropolises of the world are irrational in their stubborn reluctance to come to grips with the environmental crisis, natural and social. Idealism distorts reality because it fails to take seriously man's innate

[6] "The Just and the Sinner," *The Center Magazine*, September, 1968.

tendency to throw his best hopes to the winds and follow compulsively his natural desires for food, drink, sex, possessions, power.

On the other hand the naturalistic interpretation of man underestimates his capabilities. It minimizes his capacity to think and to dream, to create and to sacrifice, to venture and to hope. It is a matter of record that man can transcend the dimensions of nature on occasion. Socrates, Augustine, Michelangelo, Bach, Lincoln, Bonhoeffer, and Dooley, employing more than body chemistry and mechanical reflexes, fashioned philosophy, theology, art, music, responsible government, courageous dissent, and humane medicine. Biology, chemistry, physics, and behavioral psychology have contributed immeasurably to the present understanding of man and the improvement of his psychosomatic situation. But the natural sciences do not explain the man inside the man—the searching person who, clamoring for bread, refuses to be satisfied with bread alone. John Gardner observes that

> Comfort isn't enough. Ingenious diversions aren't enough. "Having enough of everything" isn't enough. If it were, the large number of Americans who have been able to indulge their whims on a scale unprecedented in history would be telling one another of their unparalleled serenity and bliss instead of trading tranquilizer prescriptions.[7]

The naturalistic interpretation of man caricatures him because it tends to see him less as a living creature with hopes and aspirations than as an inanimate object to be manipulated.

Finally, the existentialist view of man is not a full-fledged interpretation of human nature. Essentially, it is a necessary corrective in an institutionalized, auto-

[7] John W. Gardner, *No Easy Victories*, ed. Helen Rowan (New York: Harper & Row, 1968) p. 115.

mated, depersonalized culture. But existentialism, seeking the recovery of the individual, sinks its devotees in subjectivism. It recovers significant insights into the nature of man, but it does so at the expense of understanding him in depth. It is easy to complain, as Jean Paul Sartre has, that life is nauseating. It is intensely more difficult to motivate man to handle his social-political relationships responsibly. After all, it is scarcely practical—and it would be subhuman—for humanity to commit mass hara-kiri or wait resignedly for a nuclear holocaust to obliterate life!

If the rationalistic, naturalistic, and existentialist views of man fail to understand him as a whole person, what contribution does the biblical view make to our current atomistic efforts to understand man? Judeo-Christian insights speak relevantly to deep levels of man's need to understand himself and other selves.

Human nature has suffered a catastrophe. The unity of man has been broken. His freedom is despoiled. He is alienated from his fellows. This schism in human nature occurred when man, created for fellowship with God, banished his Creator from the citadel of his inner life and set up his own ego on a makeshift throne. This rebel government is unable to maintain an essential harmony in man. Each facet of his personality wars against the other facets. Paul bares this schism: "I do not do the good I want, but the evil I do not want is what I do" (Rom. 7:19 RSV). Everyman's civil war throws him into competition and conflict with his fellows, and they with him. The biblical story of man's fall—rescued from liberalism's cavalier attitude toward sin and freed from fundamentalism's refusal to differentiate myth from history—tells how man violated his freedom by rejecting God's sovereignty and fell into bondage to his own conflicting instincts, hungers, and aspirations. Man cannot break this bondage by his own will or knowledge. He cannot bridge "the ugly ditch" that he has dug between himself and God.[8] Jesus accepted this biblical description of man, declined to theorize on it, and addressed man as he is. A few years ago the "London Times Literary Supplement" observed that "the doctrine of original sin is the only empirically verifiable doctrine of the Christian Faith."

The biblical record provides massive evidence that there is a tragic flaw in man. Cain, consumed with envy, killed his brother in cold blood and then lied to save his own skin. Lust led David to scheme and to murder. Pride cost Rehoboam his kingdom. The fear of crossing a new frontier ruined Nicodemus' chance for authentic life. Simon Peter's concern for his own skin led to his denial of his Lord. Envy, bitterness, and noninvolvement nailed Jesus to the Cross. Natural man, the scriptures report matter-of-factly, is in rebellion against God, his fellows, and himself. Consequently, he denies and then appropriates the rights of others. In so doing he acts against his own interests. Man has a mercurial reason, a conscience like quicksand, a will dedicated to self and parochial interests. The doctrine of original sin reflects accurately man's actual experience of himself and other selves.

When Will Rogers was asked "What's wrong with the world anyway?" he drawled, "Well, I dunno, I guess it's people." Many middle-agers remember the pungent quip which went the rounds after World War II: "How can we have a brave new world with the same old people?" C. G. Jung warned four decades ago that modern man's civilized state was veneer; the evils of primitive man, he insisted, were crouching in

[8] James S. Whale, *Christian Doctrine* (New York: The Macmillan Co., 1941), p. 59.

the recesses of his heart. The Communist purges, the Nazi ovens, and the American napalm bombs in Vietnam burn that searing truth into human consciousness.

But these horrors cannot be attributed simply and self-righteously to the Kremlin, the Nazi Party, or the American military-industrial complex. The Russian people endured Stalin; the German industrialists, militarists, and middle class created Hitler; the affluent Americans are loath to disturb their war economy. All social problems have their roots in man. One need only look around his suburban neighborhood to see a group of children who have ganged up on a poor unfortunate playmate whom they are tormenting from sheer perversity. Reflection on this common occurrence can be stronger medicine than a fire-and-brimstone sermon. Man's inhumanity to man is concreted in the Nazi concentration camps, the tragic Dresden Fire Raid, the wanton destruction of one hundred thousand civilians in Hiroshima, and the twisted logic that decrees that villages in Vietnam must be "destroyed to save them." Carlton J. Hayes, onetime professor of European history at Columbia University, argued that every historian must acknowledge the doctrine of original sin. Whether historians acknowledge the doctrine, ignore or deny it, they do record its consequences.

Drama also, from Aeschylus to Albee—as well as history—relies on man's bent toward unpredictable evil for its most compelling themes. Without Lady Macbeth's ambition and her husband's vacillation, Shakespeare's *Macbeth* would be one dimensional. Without the bitchy wife, the indecisive husband-professor, the inanities of faculty social life in a small town college, *Who's Afraid of Virginia Woolf?* would not have taken Broadway by storm. Neither would it have attracted the expensive talents of the Burtons to the screen version.

Actors covet the roles of "bad" people; Bette Davis and Joan Crawford, Humphrey Bogart and Edward G. Robinson made screen careers of being "bad."

The human disposition to evil can be demonstrated empirically, yet modern man has not been able to reach substantial agreement on the locus of his trouble or the remedy for it. The majority continue to cling uncritically to one of the triple caricatures that man is essentially (a) rationalistic, (b) naturalistic, (c) existentialist. But their subsequent efforts to reason with man, manipulate him, or let him "do his thing" continue to lead people into blind alleys of personal frustration and society into conflict and chaos. The biblical view of man offers a unique way for him to realize his possibilities: human freedom is voluntary obedience to Christ who has demonstrated the full potential of man's splendid humanity here and now.

Jesus, accepting sin as a reality, pointed to its mysterious power. He revealed its depth, tenacity, hatefulness, and death-dealing nature. He tracked it home to the innermost part of man. By nature man is chained to self-interest. Face to face with Christ, this natural deficiency comes into sharp focus; his human pretensions are exposed in bold relief. When Christ confronts man-the-rebel and demands that his motivation conform to God's holiness, the issue is cleanly defined: no human being anywhere is able to meet that demand. There is a chasmic difference between human excellence and God's righteousness, between human sacrifice and God's sacrifice on Calvary. There are no holy men, but there can be human servants of the Holy God. Perfectionism—kissin' cousin to self-righteousness—roots in self-interest. So, the human creature is speared on his own petard. To aim at being God *is* sin. To acknowledge life's demands and accept God's authority is the ground of Christian faith which is essentially a relationship with Christ. This faith not only justifies man; it transforms him. Secular education can provide him with enlightenment on nature and society. Psychiatry can break some of his encrusted neuroses and psychoses. Statesmanship which effects realistic compromises can steady his community of political states and foster peaceful coexistence. But only God can rescue man from himself. He alone can forgive man's transgression, alienation, rebellion. God, the injured party, is the only one who can close the books on man's offenses against him and his family. And he has done that in Christ.

Modern man—like medieval, ancient, and prehistoric man—needs pardon, insight, direction, and meaning because he is mortal, finite, perverse. Man needs a new set of affections, humane goals, selfless motivation. He needs acceptance, understanding, love. "No creature in the world demands more love than man; no creature is less adapted to survive without it." [9] Burt Bacharach said that in music: "What the world needs now is love."

So we come to the essence of Christianity: "God so *loved* the world that he *gave* his only Son. . . ." It was man's desperate need for love that moved God to do what he did in Christ. It is because man cannot be truly human until he loves, and because he cannot love until he is loved, and because he cannot will to do good until he is enabled that Christians sing: "We give thee back the life we owe that in thine ocean depths its flow might richer, fuller be."

Because God wants man to be human, he sent his Son into the world in the form of a man. Having spoken through myth and legend, historical events and persons, the King finally sent his only Son. And that event turned

[9] Loren Eiseley, "An Evolutionist Looks at Modern Man," *The Immense Journey*, p. 16.

out to be the greatest act of liberation in history: it opened the way for man to recover his created humanity.

The Incarnation is cosmic response to man's lost humanity. It is because man cannot be truly human until he loves, and because he cannot love fully and freely until he is loved, and because he cannot will to do good until he is enabled to do it that Divine Love came among men in the human person of Jesus.

Paul argued from his own experience that any man who adopts God's call in Christ enters into a new form of existence: he becomes a new creature. Paul could declare, "I have run a good race, I have fought a good fight, I have kept the faith," because he faced the question which plagues Everyman, "What if I can't?" Grappling with that question, Paul admitted that he lacked the resources to do the good he wanted to do and to avoid doing the evil he deplored. But he did not decide that he had no choice. Paul responded affirmatively "to the action of One (Christ) who heals all our diseases, forgives all our iniquities, saves our lives from destruction and crowns us with everlasting mercy." [10] And in a continuing series of affirmations—acted on—Paul became a responsible human being, a new man in Christ.

Long ago, Plato remarked, "We must take the best and most irrefragable of human doctrines and embark on that as if it were a raft on which to risk the voyage of life—unless it were possible to find a stronger vessel, some Divine Word on which we might take our journey more surely and with confidence." [11]

How that "stronger vessel," the Divine Word, enables mortal man to make his journey "more surely and with confidence" is the theme of subsequent chapters.

[10] Niebuhr, *The Responsible Self,* pp. 144-45.

[11] Quoted by Loren Eiseley, *The Unexpected Universe* (New York: Harcourt Brace & World, 1969), p. 21.

*"Get to your places!" shouted the Queen in a voice of thunder, and people began running about in all directions, tumbling up against each other; however, they got settled down in a minute or two, and the game began.*

—From *Alice in Wonderland*

---

# II

# CAN ONE FIND DIRECTION IN THE SEXUAL WILDERNESS?

---

The biblical accent on the worldly nature of the gospel is currently silenced or muted in the institutional church by bureaucratic defensiveness, denominational intransigence, sectarian arrogance, and a human piety which equates the Christian life with simple decency. Denominational churchmen read John 3:16 "For God so loved the Baptists—the Presbyterians—the Catholics. . . ." Others read it: "God so loved the moralists. . . ." Middle-class churchmen in an affluent society are self-righteously convinced that it reads: "For God so loved the hardworking, successful, white Americans. . . ." These are cultural, not biblical views. For hard-pressed, searching people they obscure God's deed in Christ which was done so that the whole of his creation, responding in freedom, could be restored to harmony with his purposes. God acted as he did so that persons could be enabled to become authentically human in all their relationships.

Since sex is a human concern, we shall examine

whether biblical Christianity speaks relevantly to this dynamic strand in life. News and entertainment media and current novels have created the impression that sex is a snare only to young people and to unmarried adults.[1] But it is equally a snare for millions of married men and women between the ages of thirty and sixty. Many of them are also confused, frustrated, and humiliated by sex. It is bane or blessing for all human beings. Neither marriage nor divorce, neither sexual activity nor abstinence resolves the dilemma of sex for millions of people. Sex is an integral strand in life. It is a *human* concern.

Thomas Edwards Brown, executive coordinator, Family Life and Sex Education Council of Greater New Haven (Connecticut), acknowledging that his first formal venture in providing sex education "was a failure," explains:

> This was the crucial flaw of our initial program: driven by our own ignorance and anxiety, we failed to recognize the essential relationship of sex with sexuality, and we separated sexuality from personality. Our unwillingness to acknowledge our own sexuality had led us to detach sex from personhood and equate it solely with genital structure and functioning. We had not considered with our students how sexuality is rooted in the wholeness of personality and enmeshed in the entire fabric of feelings and relationships between persons. We had based our entire sex education program upon a fragmented and distorted concept of sex, unrealistically detached from its essential rootage in the totality of human experience. Certainly such a distortion was not intended, yet this was the result.[2]

[1] See Richard F. Hettlinger, *Living with Sex: The Student's Dilemma* (New York: Seabury Press, 1966). The title is misleading; Hettlinger discusses sex as *everyone's* dilemma.

[2] Thomas Edwards Brown, *A Guide for Christian Sex Education of Youth* (New York: Association Press, 1968), p. 26.

*Can One Find Direction in the Sexual Wilderness?*

Adults as well as adolescents, marrieds as well as unmarrieds are seeking earnestly for a way to live wholesomely with *their* sexuality.

## I

The sexual revolution, raging since World War I, had its most decisive impact during the 1960's. The decade of the 60's may well be remembered for the "Great Moral Revolution." That descriptive term rests firmly on "actualities far more pervasive than, say, the gaiety of the troubled 1890's or the elegance of the 1880's. New cosmic signs were being seen in the 1960's. The decade *did* experience a fundamental shift in American moral and religious attitudes."[3] What are the personal and social implications of this shift?

Vance Packard, a responsible reporter on social morals, decided in early 1960 to study the radically altered sexual situation in America. Expecting to complete his survey in a year or two, Professor Packard devoted almost five years to the task. His voluminous work indicates that "the great moral revolution" had left a sexual wilderness in its wake.[4] Yesterday's tried and tested roadways had been wiped out. No single code of morality could claim majority support in contemporary society. Millions of Americans roamed aimlessly and anxiously in a sexual wilderness.

This is a new strand in Western social experience. From the Reformation to the end of the nineteenth century, Protestant Europe and America were convinced—and impressed their conviction on their children—that chastity before marriage and fidelity in

[3] Sydney E. Ahlstrom, "The Radical Turn in Theology and Ethics: Why It Occurred in the 1960's," *The Annals of The American Academy of Political and Social Science*, 387, 3.

[4] Vance Packard, *The Sexual Wilderness* (New York: David McKay; 1968).

marriage are personally wholesome and socially necessary. Catholic society agreed, adding its own proviso that any interference with procreation is immoral. That was yesterday. Today, this brand of morality is spurned by many and questioned by most. Five popular views on sex in America in 1971 can be identified and described, each with a substantial bloc of subscribers, as indicated in this sketchy resume.

First, millions of Americans still cling to "Victorian morality." Narrowly moralistic, confused, desperately unhappy, and hypocritical about *their* sexuality, they are, in many cases, sex-starved people condemned to live in a sex-saturated society. Many experiment with sex angrily. These rigid, guilt-ridden people are seeking desperately to break out of their own sexual prison through conscious and unconscious acts of rebellion against an inherited "Victorian" sexual life-style. Instinctively, they sense that it is not *human.*[5]

Second, increasing numbers of Americans subscribe to a utilitarian sex ethic. "Sex for kicks" is not only popular among some teenagers, but also among many married people. A young matron has an "affair" because she is bored with suburban life. A middle-aged executive initiates an extramarital relationship because his work has gone flat. A couple, dissatisfied with their sex life, decide to swap mates with another couple. Harold Robbins and Jacqueline Susann have made a mint describing this style of sex life. It rests on an old doctrine; it is an older practice. Mechanically oriented and biologically motivated, sex without passion is dehumanizing.

Third, "recreational sex" is gaining hundreds of thousands of subscribers year after year in our affluent

[5] Rollo May, *Love and Will* (New York: W. W. Norton, 1969), pp. 67-72, provides two case studies on this.

society. This view holds that sex exists strictly for pleasure. It is a compartmentalized human activity to be enjoyed without personal involvement or personal responsibility. *Playboy* magazine popularizes this view. Its editor, Hugh Hefner, grows rich by projecting visually an ancient philosophy (hedonism), providing five and one half million moderns with vicarious excitement ("playmate" of the month) and emboldening some to find their own "playmates."

Recreational sex is also dehumanizing. By separating pleasure from purpose, it avoids authentic commitment and personal responsibility by the male to the female; this robs both of their potential humanity. Lucy Komisar, a board member of the New York Chapter of the National Organization for Women, writes: "Feminists also protest the general male proclivity to regard us as decorative, amusing sex objects even in the world outside bed. We resent the sexual sell in advertising, the catcalls we get on the street, girlie magazines and pornography. . . . Even the supposedly humanistic worlds of rock music and radical politics are not very different. Young girls who join 'the scene' or 'the movement' are labeled 'groupies' and are sexually exploited. . . ." [6]

Rollo May, calling on his rich experience in counseling, underlines another serious aspect of recreational sex.

> *Playboy* has indeed caught on to something significant in American society: Cox believes it to be "the repressed fear of involvement with women." I go farther and hold that it, as an example of the new puritanism, gets its dynamic from a repressed anxiety in American men that underlies even the fear of involvement. This is the repressed anxiety

[6] "The New Feminism," *Saturday Review*, February 21, 1970, pp. 29-30.

about impotence. Everything in the magazine is beautifully concocted to bolster the *illusion of potency* without ever putting it to the test or challenge at all. Noninvolvement (like playing it cool) is elevated into the ideal model for the Playboy. This is possible because the illusion is airtight, ministering as it does to men fearful for their potency, and capitalizing on this anxiety. The character of the illusion is shown further in the fact that the readership of *Playboy* drops off significantly after the age of thirty, when men cannot escape dealing with real women. This illusion is illustrated by the fact that Hefner himself, a former Sunday-school teacher and son of devout Methodists, practically never goes outside his large establishment in North Chicago. Ensconced there, he carries on his work surrounded by his bunnies and amidst his nonalcoholic bacchanals on Pepsi-Cola.[7]

A fourth attitude toward sex is identified, and identifies itself, with "situation ethics." Popularly dubbed the "new morality," this view calls for personal responsibility and evaluates each situation as it occurs. Rejecting legalism, it is flexible rather than rigid. It differs substantially from the other views on sex, because it takes each "situation" seriously and endorses love as the only norm. Consciously, the adherents to this view are not utilitarian; they do not seek selfish gratification.

But "the situation" and "love as the norm" are treacherous guides. Reliance on either or both without objective principles can breed injustice to others and cause unexpected pain to the practitioners. This beguiling view raises several sticky questions. Who is capable of "unselfish" love? Who is free from all neurotic tendencies? Whose finite mind can judge reliably the interrelated consequences of any human act? Who can

[7] May, *Love and Will*, pp. 58-59.

make judgments which are equally good for all the persons who are affected by any single man-woman sexual relationship? Social concern and social responsibility are casualties in the "new morality." Nonetheless, Fletcher, Robinson, and Rhymes—all churchmen—make a case for this sex style. Segments of the church, especially among the youth, endorse it. Many university and military chaplains lean toward it. An increasing number of pastoral counselors in the parishes approve it.[8]

Fifth, there is the homosexual style among males and females. Other societies have been tolerant of this style for centuries, but American society has been secretive, suspicious, and condemnatory toward it until recently. During the 60's, a serious concern for the homosexual as a person and a humane desire to understand him (her) emerged in some quarters. The change is easily discernible. A decade ago Rex Harrison and Richard Burton would have refused flatly to portray two aging homosexuals in a motion picture which attracted millions of viewers in 1969, scarcely a vintage year in the movie industry. Films like *The Fox, The Killing of Sister George,* and *Staircase* could not have been produced during the 1950's. The climate of American opinion has undergone a radical change concerning the homosexual. *Time,* October 31, 1969, gave its cover and feature story to the avowed advocates and practitioners of this sex style. The current debate turns on whether homosexuality is a disease to be treated or a way of life to be accepted among adults. Counselors differ on that issue, but they endorse the new openness and honesty that allows a compassionate concern for

[8] See Joseph Fletcher, *Moral Responsibility: Situation Ethics at Work* (Philadelphia: Westminster Press, 1967), chapter V; and *Storm Over Ethics* (Philadelphia: United Church Press, 1967), especially chapters 2, 4, and 5.

the homosexual as a person.[9] But can homosexuality ever be the fullest *human* expression of sexuality?

At the end of the 1960's, it was evident that a sexual wilderness existed. Yesterday's guideposts were gone. Youth *and* their parents were wandering in a sexual wilderness and increasing numbers admitted to being lost in the wasteland. Mechanical sex, utilitarian sex, recreational sex, situational sex, and homosexuality had claimed millions of Americans who appeared to be engaging in more sex and enjoying it less!

Unquestionably, there had been a qualitative change in the moral climate of opinion and behavior in Western society. At the close of the 1950's, the cultural analyst, Pitirim Sorokin, concluded that the American sex revolution had set the stage for a "listless drift towards sex anarchy." In 1969, the compassionate Rollo May declared flatly

> that our highly-vaunted sexual freedom has turned out to be a new form of puritanism. I spell it with a small "p" because I do not wish to confuse this with original Puritanism. That, as in the passion of Hester and Dimmesdale in Hawthorne's *The Scarlet Letter*, was a very different thing. I refer to puritanism as it came down via our Victorian grandparents and became allied with industrialism and emotional and moral compartmentalization.
>
> I define this puritanism as consisting of three elements. First, *a state of alienation from the body*. Second, *the separation of emotion from reason*. And third, *the use of the body as a machine*. . . .
>
> Thus it is not surprising that, as sex becomes more machinelike, with passion irrelevant and then even pleasure diminishing, the problem has come full circle. And we find, *mirabile dictu*, a progression from an *anesthetic* attitude to an *antiseptic* one. Sexual contact itself then tends to get

[9] See Fletcher, *Moral Responsibility*, pp. 92-111. See also *The Wolfenden Report* (London: Macmillan & Co., 1963).

put on the shelf and to be avoided. This is another and surely least constructive aspect of the new puritanism: it returns, finally, to a new asceticism. This is said graphically in a charming limerick that seems to have sprung up on some sophisticated campus:

The word has come down from the Dean
That with the aid of the teaching machine,
King Oedipus Rex
Could have learned about sex
Without ever touching the Queen.[10]

## *II*

In a radically changed and kaleidoscopically changing social milieu, did the Christian church offer meaningful guidelines as it had for centuries?

The Catholic Church struggled valiantly to do so, but Pope Paul VI, clinging to his church's official view, failed to persuade suburban housewives, bachelor girls, the jet set, the poor, and many of his clergy in the Dutch and American churches. Soliloquizing in the encyclical, *Humanae Vitae,* Paul appeared as an ecclesiastical Hamlet to some and an anti-Galileo churchman to others. Widespread dissent on this and other social issues threatens to split the Catholic Church.

The Protestant Church in its approach to sex, love, marriage, family life, and divorce also failed to provide relevant guidance for youth and many adults, married or unmarried. This massive confusion in Protestant circles was focused in the early 1960's by a courageous statement on sex from the English Quakers.[11] While the framers of the Quaker view stated that they did not speak for all the Quakers of England (and certainly not for all

[10] May, *Love and Will,* pp. 45 and 61.
[11] *Towards a Quaker View of Sex,* rev. ed., Alastair Heron, ed. (London: Friends Home Service Committee, Friends House, 1964).

Protestants), most Christians agreed with some conclusions in the Report. Here are several which enjoy wide support. There is no private morality; every human act (moral, immoral, amoral) has social implications as well as personal implications. "However private an act, it is never without its impact on society. . . ."[12] Many Christians agree with that conclusion. Second, the family is the cornerstone of society. In spite of the mounting critiques of the family, Protestant, Catholic, and Orthodox teaching supports this conclusion. Third, no person should be exploited by any other person. All Christians endorse *that,* at least in theory. But when the Quaker view states categorically that there are situations when premarital sex is more wholesome than chastity and extramarital sex is more responsible than fidelity, a substantial bloc of Protestants, Roman Catholics, and Orthodoxists dissent vigorously. Nonetheless, it is clear that a widening climate of permissiveness in sexual behavior is abroad in the church.

A sexual wilderness exists. The guideposts of yesteryear are gone. The church itself mirrors the confusion, uncertainty, and "lostness" which characterize society in general. It has failed to offer meaningful guidance to millions of hard-pressed moderns in complex social situations. Church members, like nonmembers, have been pretty much on their own since 1950.

## III

Is the sexual wilderness unique to this era? Some think not. They point first to the Bible's earthy view of sex. From the creation myth to Paul's unvarnished directives, scripture is indeed forthright about sex. Cecil B. DeMille, in the heyday of Hollywood, could not resist the David and Bathsheba story; translated to the

[12] *Ibid.,* p. 40.

screen, it was a surefire money-maker. Hollywood's motives and its treatment of biblical stories may be suspect, but scripture does present sex as an integral strand in life and a volatile force in human history.

Secular history also records that other societies and eras were remarkably freewheeling in sexual affairs. The Romans in the days of the Empire were vigorous sex-activists; one Empress kept score on her nightly extra-marital escapades. Augustine, before his conversion to Christianity, was a regular client of the brothels in Alexandria. The *Canterbury Tales* and *Decameron* reveal that the Middle Ages had its sexual wilderness as well as its monasteries, cathedrals, and crusades. The medieval theologian Abelard was forcibly deprived of part of his anatomy for sleeping with Eloise who in turn was banished to a nunnery for being cooperative. Eighteenth century France had many DuBarrys, none of whom was a lady. Bundling in Puritan New England was not as innocent as some high school history texts imply. Social historians estimate that one in three Puritan couples had premarital sex. But the Puritans did not separate sex from passion and love. They had an earthy respect for it as a human concern.

Nonetheless, close examination suggests that there is a *qualitative* difference between the social climate in our era and in other periods of history. This radical change of climate which affects the styles of sex today stems from a radically different social situation. Widespread affluence and leisure, provided by an industrial-urban society, are new strands in social history. Never have so many people had so much money and so much free time, both of which are necessary for sexual experimentation before and after marriage. Heretofore, only the leisure class had multiple opportunities to experiment widely with sex. Today, millions of people have the leisure, mobility, and economic means to "sleep around."

Further, an industrial-urban society provides anonymity which is necessary for sexual experimentation on a broad scale. Yesterday's rural communities and small towns were social fishbowls. Local customs, town gossips, and ingrained pretense combined to erect strong barriers against sexual experimentation. It occurred, of course, but not widely nor openly. Pre-urban American communities were towns without pity. But "Middletown, America" is vanishing. Affluence, leisure, anonymity, and mobility (economic and geographic)—social by-products of the urban-industrial society—have created a new social situation in which sexual freedom among females and males flourishes (bachelor apartments, weekend ski parties, office parties, etc.). Two generations ago the mass production of the automobile, a mobile bedroom, had provided sexual privacy to many people at all economic levels. Finally, modern medicine's effective control of pregnancy and venereal disease in the 1960's further liberated the female and emboldened the male, if they availed themselves of these medical services.

These new social factors (affluence, leisure, anonymity, mobility, permissiveness, and science) make the current situation for sexual experimentation *qualitatively* different from what it was in other eras of history. This difference comes into focus when one compares Victorian women, who boasted of their frigidity or experienced guilt over their natural sex feelings, with Modern women, whose conversations on sex in mixed groups are so candid that many of them become frustrated because they aren't enjoying sex the way their neighbors say it should be enjoyed! American society is sex-saturated. TV commercials advise brunettes and redheads that "blondes have more fun." A sultry-voiced female, cooing suggestively, "Take it all off," entices males to purchase a particular brand of shaving cream. Films like *The Adventurers* and *Myra Breckinridge* suggest that our sex-saturated society is actually a sex-starved society. Best-selling books like *The Love Machine, Naked Came the Stranger,* and *The Sensuous Woman* support that judgment. The current social situation is *qualitatively* different from what it was in preceding eras of history.

## *IV*

Since an accepted church teaching on sex does not exist, concerned Christians are now forced to examine freshly the biblical view of sex and love and personal responsibility. This is salutary, hopeful. Responsible churchmen—working from the biblical frame of reference, confronting realistically the diverse views on sex which currently attract and captivate church members as well as nonmembers, dialoguing with people where they are, and examining critically the views of specialists (counselors, psychiatrists, sociologists)—will participate in the crucial search for a humane morality for persons who want to celebrate sex responsibly. There are several *biblical guidelines* for an immediate involvement with adolescents and adults who want authentic sex as an integral strand in their rich human experience.

1. God creates, redeems, and inspirits people to be truly human. The Christian God is not a rule-maker. He is not a cosmic policeman who "shadows" people and keeps a secret file on their private deeds. The Christian God is a Father who, desiring fellowship, creates male and female children to relate meaningfully to him and to one another in all human acts—worship, work, lovemaking, procreation, family life, politics, and leisure.

These persons, fashioned in God's image (person), have the capacity to relate to one another with respect, understanding, responsibility, love, and sacrifice. Biblical religion, interpreted in the light of Christ's teaching, makes it plain that God intends men and women to accept sex joyously and unashamedly in a voluntarily pledged relationship of fidelity based on expected and projected permanency.

Both the Old Testament witness in Genesis and the New Testament teachings of Christ support this view of human sexuality as a good aspect of God's creation, leading to the conjugal relationship in which men and women can find mutual completion. It is important to note in this regard that the word "flesh" is used in Scripture to refer not only to the skin covering our bodies, but to the whole of man's being—body and personality together as one entity. The concept of unity in "one flesh" is to be understood not simply as a bodily union of male and female, but as a total union of two whole human beings, two complete selves in a relationship of mutuality.[13]

When God became a man born of woman—"the Word was made flesh"—he demonstrated concretely his rejection of any ontology which views the body as "evil" and the spirit as "good." Man is not a disembodied spirit; neither is he only a body. The Incarnation and the Resurrection rest upon and confirm the wholeness of human personhood.

Some of Christ's followers in the early centuries of the church allowed their personal judgment to cloud this many-splendored truth. Augustine, more than others, introduced the view that sex is evil. He taught that original sin is transferred from generation to generation through the act of sex and that coitus in marriage is

[13] Brown, *A Guide for Christian Sex Education of Youth*, p. 95.

sinful unless conception is intended. Tragically, Augustine's view became an accepted strand in Christian tradition. Popularly, his view came to mean, "sex is evil," "sex is dirty," "virginity is good," "sexual self-denial is more holy than marriage." These views contradict the biblical view of sex as a wondrous gift from God which, claimed in mutual love and fidelity in the context of shared responsibility and expected permanency, ennobles and fulfills persons. For too long, too many "Christians" have acted as though God had made a mistake when he created us male and female! A vigorous recovery of the biblical view will correct this cultural estimate, which is in fact neurotic. Responsible churchmen will orient boldly and aggressively to the biblical view of sex and accept the consequences of that stance in a moralistic church and a neurotic society. Christ came to enable men and women to recover their whole humanity and experience life abundantly.

2. Second, biblical religion accepts man realistically as a complex of appetites, desires, hungers. Man needs food and physical comfort. He desires love, companionship, and recognition. He hungers for security and meaning. These appetites are part of man's natural inheritance. If he allows these natural desires to run wild or represses them negatively, they will flaw his humanity. Jesus' directive for handling all human hungers creatively is voluntary self-discipline. Christians are identifiable not by their intellectual subscription to accepted dogmas, but by their serious efforts to discipline their natural appetites as a consequence of their willing obedience to Christ. "Why call ye me, 'Lord, Lord,' and do not my commandments?" The biblical view is unequivocal: freedom *is* obedience to Christ. That is the "narrow gate" through which man enters to claim his full humanity.

Human hungers (food, shelter, sex, love, recognition, and meaning) are given to fulfill essential human purposes and provide splendid human pleasures. The "giver" is God himself. Perhaps this phrase, "pleasure and purpose," can clarify our thinking here.[14] Man's desires are given by God for man's pleasure and purpose. Man becomes truly human only when purpose *and* pleasure are brought into equilibrium in his person. For example, healthy humans enjoy a good meal. Jesus' enemies accused him of being "a wine-bibber and a gluttonous man." *Bon appetit* is a holy wish to any human being. It is also necessary that man eat to live. Physical hunger alerts him to that physiological necessity. But, if man isolates purpose from pleasure—if he lives to eat—he is less than human; and if he isolates pleasure from purpose—if he eats only to live—he is also less than human.

Of course, man needs other material goods to live comfortably. And God has provided these for his disciplined use or endowed him with the imagination and will to "create" them from the raw materials in God's created world. To exist with dignity, civilized man now requires more "material" things than he did in a primitive culture. That is also part of God's intention for man so long as he does not manipulate or exploit other humans or impoverish God's order of nature or glut himself to provide these creature comforts. Man also needs religion, art, music, literature, and philosophy to be fully human. These lift human existence into meaningful experience. But again, if the pleasure provided by any one of them becomes an end in itself, if his preoccupation with "possession" (a Cezanne or a sports

[14] I am indebted to Walter Kerr, New York *Times*' drama critic, for this phrase.

car, for example) smothers responsible stewardship, man's humanness is warped, society is disrupted, and the natural order is thrown out of balance. Man's hungers for food, shelter, security, recognition, sex, love, and meaning are inescapable drives in his personal and social experience. His humanity is maimed when either purpose or pleasure becomes the overriding drive in fulfilling any of these natural hungers. Authentic celebration of life requires the balance of these.

3. God created man with freedom of choice in all areas of intimate human experience. Obviously, man's socio-economic-political situation delimits his freedom in varying degrees. A black youth in suburban Cleveland enjoys a larger freedom than an Indian threatened with extermination in northern Brazil. But every human being is free to resist or rebel in any social situation if he is willing to pay the price as Socrates, Jesus, Augustine, Hus, Thomas More, William Barclay, Roger Williams, Washington, Lincoln, and Bonhoeffer did. Man's personal freedom is limited substantially by the web of human association, time, and space; but his freedom to decide personal issues for himself is never wholly obliterated, even in a concentration camp. The human spirit remains essentially free in every situation to attach itself, by decision or default, to whomever and whatever it will.

By nature, human beings are erratic in exercising this freedom. External disciplines are necessary.[15] But discipline without freedom ends in tyranny even as freedom without discipline ends in anarchy. Ancient Israel, free from Egyptian bondage, required strong external disciplines to guarantee order and insure justice in their new society: thou shalt not kill; thou shalt not

[15] See James T. Laney, "Norm and Context in Ethics: A Reconsideration," *Soundings*, LII (Autumn, 1969), 311-22.

commit adultery; thou shalt not steal; thou shalt not bear false witness. In the biblical view of personal and social life, the primary issue is not whether a deed is right or wrong but whether it is sane or insane, constructive or destructive, authentic or inauthentic, orderly or chaotic, just or unjust, person-centered or thing-centered, God-oriented or ego-oriented.

Several mundane illustrations will support this argument. Traffic laws can be irksome. But if all traffic laws were rescinded and all law enforcers were retired from service, chaos and carnage would result. Professional football would be a shambles without rules and officials to interpret them. A Boy Scout camp without rules would be bedlam. A factory assembly line without safety regulations would be a slaughter house. Man, a complex of appetites and aspirations, never outgrows his need for internal and external disciplines if he is to be whole and his society is to be stable and just.

Obviously, some people need firmer external disciplines than others. Parents learn that quickly. One child requires firm external disciplines while another does not. One internalizes principles readily; the other does not. This is equally true of adults. Social justice rests on reasonable restraints equitably administered with the enlightened consent of the majority and the persistent review by the minority. Responsible dissent keeps the majority alert and sensitive to the changing need for laws which allow all people an equal opportunity to be human. Social grace depends on individuals who relate charitably and concernedly to their fellow humans. Those who accept Jesus' demands and claim his promises take on his humanity. These "new" humans work to devise political, economic, and social structures which insure and foster social justice. They also share God's love with persons.

No human deed then is ever wholly private. Every personal decision, acted on, has social consequences. Each private deed has a public impact. When two seventeen-year-olds, strongly attracted to one another, insist that they be allowed to marry, they rarely admit their personal inexperience to handle sex and love creatively or marriage and family responsibly. Challenged on these points, they bristle, arguing that it is *their* right to marry if *they* please. But is it ever that simple?

When a thirty-eight-year-old married man and a thirty-three-year-old woman, sexually attracted to each other, decide to divorce their respective mates and marry, that private decision has public consequences. An incontrovertible mark of emotional maturity for and in marriage is the developed human capacity to see and accept marriage as a social contract as well as a private agreement between two human beings. Marriage vows are personal and private; their implications are social and public. The ability to perceive that is one proof of a couple's readiness for marriage.

4. Since, as we noted above, biblical religion underscores the reality that man is endowed by God with appetites intended for purpose and pleasure, it also affirms that he is so fashioned that he is fragmented, frustrated, if he allows either to become an end in itself. That is man's built-in "fail-safe" system. The human desire to acquire, undisciplined, becomes avarice which tarnishes persons and disrupts society (the "Robber Barons," 1870–1900). The human desire for recognition, undisciplined, exhausts talent and disturbs society (Marilyn Monroe). The human desire for power, undisciplined, crushes individuals and wreaks social havoc (Hitler, Stalin). The human desire to cohabit, undisciplined, despoils persons and disorders

society (the "sexual wilderness"). Earning a livelihood, acquiring property, winning professional recognition, making love—these human drives provide man with pleasure and purpose. Inexorably, they breed sorrow and frustration if they are repressed or given undisciplined rein. That is a firm strand in biblical Christianity. It is also the essence of human experience.

## V

A responsible church—admitting that many of its members are lost in the sexual wilderness, cognizant that various sex styles co-exist, concerned that life shall be humane, and working to accept the authority of the God of love and righteousness—will engage in honest dialogues between and among the advocates of all sex styles in the hope that a *humane* morality can be fashioned for persons who want to celebrate the gift of sex responsibly.

Questions like these can be used as openers in any discussion group.

1. If one is "Victorian"—rigid, moralistic, guilt-ridden—in his attitude toward sex, should he engage in sex as a means to break out of his prison? Are the affirmative suggestions of some counselors on this escape helpful or hurtful?

2. If one endorses utilitarian sex, should he proceed uncritically or examine with a counselor what happens to persons in the process?

3. If one is hooked on "recreational sex," should he go from bunny to bunny, coed to coed, bed to bed in suburbia and on the road? Should he examine whether the personal disciplines he exercises in his business, professional, or academic life; his use of alcohol, automobile, money, etc., are equally applicable in his sex

life? Is untrammeled freedom in *any* life situation likely to maim one's person and disrupt society? Can freedom and discipline be balanced in one's person? Can they be brought into social equilibrium? Why bother?

4. If one endorses "situation ethics" should he, "loving" his secretary, negate his vow to his wife and children to foster the "new" relationship? Is adultery ever wholesome as some theologians suggest? [16] Is there an essential difference between premarital and extramarital sex? Are there personal risks in premarital sex? Is any human relationship wholly private, totally without social impact? Is monogamy outdated?

5. If one is homosexual, or inclines to this style of sex, should he (she) seek psychiatric help or lobby for laws which allow consenting adults to engage in any sexual experience they desire?

> Sex is dynamite. Unchanneled by high character it leads to chaos and destruction. It can be the fiercest cement of relationship, but it can also be the lever that breaks people apart. Conceived broadly as "libido" it is the most "dynamic" of assets as a means to good ends, including love as well as procreation. Our danger is that while technology (medical and industrial) makes intercourse easier, our moral *ability* to serve our ideals has not kept pace. The ideal no longer finds support in the "facts of life." This is what is called the moral lag, a religious and moral (not scientific) problem. It is much like the new atomic energy: science gives us the new power, but to what end will we use it? For better living, or for self-destruction? [17]

If the church is seriously concerned to help people celebrate sex responsibly, it will take its good news that

[16] Fletcher, *Situation Ethics* (Philadelphia: Westminster Press, 1966), pp. 163-65. Two actual situations, "Christian Cloak and Dagger" and "Sacrificial Adultery," are described by Professor Fletcher.

[17] Fletcher, *Moral Responsibility*, p. 91.

man can be human into the bedrooms of the city, suburbs, the country side, and the college dormitories, as well as into the marketplace and the political arena, and will dialogue openly but firmly from the resources of the Word (Christ) with people *where they are, as they are.* Jesus dispersed the self-righteous accusers of the woman taken in adultery. He forgave her unreservedly. He also told her: "Go and *sin* no more."

*I have need of others who*
*have need of me and of*
*each other.*

—Albert Camus

*But when love suddenly springs up when we least expect it—love for a hostile individual substituted for the natural aggressive riposte, prompting forgiveness, displacing self-interest—then we are in the presence of a creative act that is really free and undetermined. It is a bursting forth of life, a positive choosing of a new direction, breaking the chain of natural reactions.*

—Paul Tournier

# III

# CAN THE GENERATION GAP BE BRIDGED?

Christ was not crucified between two candlesticks on an altar in a cathedral but between two thieves on a barren hill next to the garbage dump outside Jerusalem.[1] Jesus—born in a cow shed, reared in poverty, soul brother to the dispossessed and the oppressed—was murdered because he prodded men to accept responsibility for each other regardless of race, creed, and color. He was "worldly" in every sense except one, nonconformity to material goals and values; he considered persons to be of inestimable value to God and to one another. But in the sense that Jesus was worldly,

[1] George McLeod provides this "mind-blowing" reminder.

contemporary white and black church members are not; and in the sense that he was "unworldly," they are not. The majority are content to be role-players (pretenders) at home as well as in the marketplace, the political arena, and the church. That is one searing reason (among many) why serious-minded young people reject the values and goals of contemporary society.

One strand in the hypocrisy of many parents toward their children is that they do not relate wholesomely to one another as mates, pretending to the public meantime that all is well. This debilitating dishonesty undermines teen-agers' confidence in their parents and distorts their expectations for marriage and family life.

Another strand in the hypocrisy which separates the generations is woven by the news media. Their preoccupation with bizarre events creates the impression that most young people are "taking trips," arranging sex orgies, breaking down ivy-covered walls, and plotting to overthrow the government. Many adults, accepting these reports uncritically, view all young people suspiciously. It is likely that this unbalanced reporting also prompts emotionally insecure youth to rebel simply because they consider it the "in" thing to do. Keeping up with one's peers is not confined to Establishment middle-agers.

An additional facet in the hypocrisy which ruins trust between the generations is fashioned by a segment of youth who are *not* bent on reform. Their purpose is ill-defined, their honesty is thin, their motives are shoddy. Young people are human, too. Like adults, some youth claim freedom without assuming responsibility; they confuse license with liberty. There is a small sector of young people whose drug usage, recreational and utilitarian sex activities, rebellion against academic disciplines for the sake of rebellion, and avoidance of social and political responsibilities are the results of doing what comes naturally. They never rise above this level of escapism and negativism. Some of these are, as Nathan Pusey of Harvard observed in mid-1970, "Joe McCarthys" in reverse. Their leftist tactics are as dehumanizing as McCarthy's totalitarian rightist tactics were in the early 1950's.

Finally, any appraisal of the "generation gap" is hypocritical if it deliberately ignores the millions of homes in class-stratified America where the gap is not chasmic, where communication has not broken down. In these homes there are hard differences between the generations and ugly moments of hostility, as there are between mates in the strongest marriages, but a chasmic gap has not resulted. In fact, maturing relationships exist in tension between the generations in some American homes, schools, churches and communities. The aim in this presentation is first to understand and then to get at ways to help young people and adults separated by a wide gap, where hostility divides, where alienation destroys. This "gap" is a serious social problem at all levels in American society.

## *I*

To a degree, the generation gap is inevitable because it is inherent in life. It need not be chasmic, but it is as natural as death. Adults and youth must work to bridge it. Over the years, adults incline to be less open and less adaptable to change. Their emotional structures become rigid; they accept the status quo more readily. They endure the ambiguous present and idealize the chaotic past. Meanwhile, the younger generation —seeking their identity as persons—demand personal freedom, independence to make judgments, and acceptance of their right to do "their thing." Conflict is natural. Further, in a society where geriatrics is an effective branch of medicine, the generation gap becomes three dimensional.

When former Supreme Court Justice, Oliver Wendell Holmes, in his nineties at the time, advised President Franklin Roosevelt that he was reading Plato to improve his mind, Holmes was light years ahead of many of today's senior citizens living in colonies in Florida and Southern California and scattered through many communities. In contrast with Holmes who kept moving toward new horizons, most retirees gloat over their investments or lament their economic hardships; they indulge in sweeping criticisms of youth, blacks, poverty-imprisoned whites, and public welfare; they deplore taxes, communism, America's military stalemate, foreign aid, and socially involved churchmen; they laud the supposed "character-building" effect of the Great Depression. Justice Holmes would have been repelled by these people. It is natural that young people, straining after independence and eager to experiment, collide not only with authority figures (parents, teachers, clergy, policemen) but also infuriate these oldsters. Tension among three generations is inevitable.

Scripture is crammed with accounts of conflict between the generations. Jonathan turned his back on his father Saul. King David suffered a full-scale military rebellion at the hands of his ambitious son, Absalom. Mary and Joseph spent three anxious days looking for their other-oriented twelve-year-old "lost" in the city of Jerusalem.

Secular history, too, is filled with examples of the generation gap. Socrates complained bitterly about the young people of his day. Marcus Aurelius fathered the unworthy Commodus. Luther's father disapproved his son's choice of a vocation. Lord and Lady Randolph Churchill did not relate meaningfully to their late-blooming son, Winston Spencer. Mrs. John Eisenhower, a religious pacifist, grieved when her son, Dwight David, entered West Point. John and Robert Kennedy discarded their father's political conservatism.

Literature also leans heavily on the generation gap for dynamic themes. *King Lear* is one long gap between father and children. Dickens' *Christmas Carol* relies on the theme. Dostoevsky's *The Brothers Karamazov* depicts bitter differences between the generations. Certainly the classic on the generation gap is Jesus' story of the Prodigal Son.

The "gap" crops up every two decades; it is as certain as death and taxes. But in this era it is qualitatively different. Today, there is a new dimension to the age-old collision between the generations.

## *II*

One reason for this qualitative difference is the widening chasm between the generations' approach to knowledge. When I attended college, I learned to be critical, evaluative, "objective." Exposed to documentary sources on the first World War, I discovered how Britain and France had played on American sympathies by maligning Germany. When I shared this "new" knowledge with my father, he advised me curtly that I was misinformed. He had *experienced* World War I. He *knew* the Germans caused the war. My father was pitting his subjective (existential) judgment against my objective (historical) judgment. Today, many young people are doing precisely what my father did. Subjective judgment is not an invention of the "now" generation.

But is existential knowledge any more dependable

than historical knowledge? The conflict between these ways of "knowing" is acute today because both youth and adults absolutize: subjectivism *or* objectivism, existentialism *or* historicism, value *or* fact. The exclusive employment of either approach distorts reality. It is one facet of the collisional difference between the two generations' approach to knowledge.[2] There is another.

Sensitive young people are disenchanted with the "objectivism" of our generation. They observed us analyzing and criticizing only to see most of us go along finally to get along materially. Our generation recognized the problems of a dehumanized society. Fiction and nonfiction in the 1930's and 40's and 50's document that fact. *Grapes of Wrath* (poverty), *The Man in the Gray Flannel Suit* and *The Organization Man* (the corporation world), *The Caine Mutiny* (the military), *The Crisis in the University* (education), *The Affluent Society* (material goals), etc., are examples of pungent social criticism before and after World War II. Further, many scientists, philosophers, editors, and clergymen (Oppenheimer, Russell, Cousins, Bennett) dedicated themselves to the task of outlawing nuclear war. Our generation had battalions of competent social analysts and several squads of prophets. But neither they nor we took imaginative, bold action to improve the human situation. We analyzed until our wills were paralyzed. We aimed at the moon more vigorously than we aimed at racism, urban ghettoes, suburban boredom, and international poverty. And what we aimed at we achieved. But our youth were not impressed!

Perceptive young people have lost patience with our intellectual critiques, outmoded traditions, and grad-

[2] The current disposition to absolutize the "objective" or "subjective" ways of knowing has divided philosophers, theologians, and politicians as well as youth, parents, and teachers.

ualism. They ACT. They reject the "action" in Vietnam and organize peace demonstrations and seek to get peace candidates elected to public office. They criticize bureaucratic education and participate in tutoring projects, etc. They ignore "service-club" churches and engage in serious religious discussions on their own. They disdain social critiques, philosophies, and theologies which speak only to an in-group of professionals or an insulated social class. Young people today are not linear thinkers. They think with their guts: "The ABM is an Edsel"; "Make love, not war"; "Tell it like it is." Our generation must accept their massive impatience penitently but not uncritically. Thinking with one's blood can be as dangerous as detached thinking disassociated from action. The generations need each other desperately. Each can help the other. Together, they may accomplish salutary social changes. But before that cooperation can be forged the older generation must come to understand the young generation. Margaret Mead is right: anyone born before 1944 is an immigrant! Young people 15–26 know only the world of nuclear weapons, the cold war, Vietnam, racial strife, emerging new nations, campus unrest, moonshots, organ transplants, TV, frozen foods, sport cars, jet planes, permissiveness, *et al.* People over twenty-six are immigrants in this strange world; many are not able to adapt to the ways of this new world. This qualitative difference in cultural experience drives a wedge between the generations.

Today's youth have known only a *sensate* culture. All cultures, of course, are sensate in the degree that people see, hear, touch, taste, and smell, but the bombardment of the human senses in this generation has brought a new dimension to society in the last quarter century. In former generations, for example, smell was identified with food, city streets, new-mown lawns, open fields, and barnyards. Now, the focus is on *how* one smells. If the male uses a particular after-shave lotion, he is advised that he will find it necessary to beat off a bevy of beautiful females. If the female uses a particular perfume, she is assured that she will devastate all males. The implication is that the quality of personhood (character, intelligence, compassion) is incidental to the smell one has! A thoroughly sensate culture externalizes and mechanizes human relationships. Today, many children (and wives) are incensed if the head of the household cannot provide two cars, and preferably three, like the three chairs for the three bears. Millions of young people demand and get their own cars. When dispossessed people looted during the riots of the sixties they evidenced as much interest in color TV sets as in food and clothing. The human appetite for additional material goods is whetted by TV, fed by installment buying, and guaranteed by built-in obsolescence. The difference between the generations' expectations is qualitative in today's sensate culture.

Second, young people have been reared in a thoroughly *secular* culture. Inescapably, all civilized people have lived in a secular (worldly) culture, but presently secularism is the dominant life style; for most people, there is no other. "Will it work?" "Will it succeed?" "Will it sell?" are the questions that count. Creative imagination is rare in government. Idealism is thin in public education. The Cross is avoided in church. Secularism (the pragmatic, the successful, the material) has surfeited the "now" generation. In spite of rhetoric and jargon, bureaucratic government, corporations, institutional Christianity, public education, and family relationships are thoroughly secularized. Land on the moon; sell the product; meet the benevolence quota; get the A or B in the academic community; own a suburban home—these are the goals in our secular society. To achieve them most people employ any means and justify any method that gets results. This absolutized secular culture has seeped into every crevice of youth's daily experience. Presently, a minority of the youth are in open rebellion against these secular values and goals. They disdain our "junk culture" and despise our hypocritical oratory. But the majority of young people are preparing to claim their share in it.

Third, young people experience a culture which accepts uncritically *science* as Truth and as a society-changing technology. Our generation grew up in a culture on the edge of scientism. We looked on science as a benevolent uncle, not as a consuming demon. In our formative years, Buck Rogers was a romantic figure in a cartoon strip. Our children *know* that "Buck Rogers" lives in Houston with a wife and 2.6 kids and has a name like the neighbors'—Carpenter, Shepard, Armstrong, Gordon, Bean, Lovell. It has become impossible even for the specialists and educators to keep pace with science these days. Ninety-five percent of the scientists who ever lived on the earth are alive today! The socio-economic implications of science as a society-changing technology are incalculable.

A decade ago when commercial jet service was introduced, the flight engineer, indispensable on the four-engine prop planes, lost his job. Technology had made his vocation obsolete. During the last decade, miners, factory workers, laborers, and skilled workers got up morning after morning to find themselves and their skills unwanted in an automated society. New jobs and positions are created by the new technology, but many displaced workers cannot qualify for them.

The social-psychological-economic impact of the "knowledge explosion" has been immeasurable in the last several decades. Meantime, our political, educational, and religious institutions lack a style flexible enough to adapt to the social changes effected by the knowledge explosion in science and technology. This lag in social institutions has bewildered, disheartened, and alienated many youth. Roszac's *Counter Culture* appeals to some young people, but it has not captivated most of them by any means.

Electronics demonstrates this point vividly. TV's instant view provides vicarious involvement in contemporary events. Its psycho-social impact is incalculable. When the older generation attended movies like *What Price Glory?* and *Wings*, their personal involvement was minimal. They knew that Victor McLaughlin, Edmund Lowe, Richard Arlen, and Buddy Rogers were actors. They did not confuse the "play" with reality. Today twelve-year-olds, via the tube, experience emotional shock, in some cases traumatic, from the violence and dehumanization they witness on the battlefields of Vietnam and along the Arab-Israeli border. They see war for what it is: destruction, degradation, death. Understandably, sensitive and intelligent young people reject the chauvinistic nationalism which has claimed an uncritical generation of Legionnaires and Veterans of Foreign Wars. The My Lai Massacre, the ritual of "the body count," the racist disdain for the Vietnamese suggest that the young people have been right from the beginning in calling America's war "imperialist."

Today's youth have instant knowledge of and vicarious participation in the violence in our cities, the poverty in Appalachia, the war in Vietnam, the moonlandings, and underwater research. The qualitative difference between their experience and ours is so profound that professional counselors, imaginative teachers, and responsible parents often fail in their efforts to acquaint young people with the ambiguities of history and the tragic strand in human life. Adults have made a beginning at bridging the gap when they realize that the responsibility to teach young people is linked inextricably with the privilege of learning from them. In earlier generations the immigrants who adapted best learned from their children. At the same time, the children who profited most learned basic values from their immigrant parents. But a two-way learning experience depends partially on the ability of both generations to listen. Many people, young and old, are willing to listen but few are skilled in this complex process. Listening is an art. Karl Menninger puts it this way:

> Listening is a magnetic and strange thing, a creative force. The friends who listen to us are the ones we move toward, and we want to sit in their radius. When we are listened to, it creates us, makes us unfold and expand. I tell myself to listen with affection to anyone who talks to me. This person is showing me his soul. It is a little dry and meager and full of grinding talk just now, but soon he will begin to think. He will show his true self; will be wonderfully alive.[3]

It is crucial that each generation listen "with affection" to the other. Parent to child, child to parent, mate to mate, brother to sister, sister to brother, friend to friend, adversary to adversary, each must listen "with affection" if the widening chasms between persons are to be bridged. In an age when sound is fury, noise is bedlam, and words are discordant sounds (not deeds), people

[3] Karl Menninger, *Love Against Hate* (New York: Harper & Row, 1967), p. 143.

hear, but they do not listen. Too many in both generations—defensive for their own views, self-righteous, doctrinaire—are unwilling to entertain any other viewpoint than their own. Consequently, the channels of effective communication are closed. The current generation gap is only one evidence of this psycho-social crisis in American life. The crisis is crippling the churches, the schools, and the government as adults also refuse to dialogue with one another on controversial issues.

## *III*

What are the "young radicals" critical of? First, it is necessary to discover who the critics are and to get a reasonable estimate of their numerical strength. The overly publicized "young radicals" are not in the majority. Many adults accept uncritically the news stories, magazine articles, and TV presentations which give the impression that most young people are (a) insurrectionists, (b) junkies, (c) first-stage alcoholics, and (d) constant experimenters with sex.

Nothing could be less true. A substantial number of young people *experiment* with marijuana, heroin, or LSD; but it is a minority who are addicted. A substantial bloc of people insist on a private sex ethic (which is not new), yet a refreshing number are intensely serious in their desire to establish meaningful man-woman relationships.[4] Actually, many young people are retreating into privatism.[5] It is clear that the majority intend to get their education, join the establishment (business, education, religion), seek advancement, and work for material security. The "four horse-

[4] Erich Segal's *Love Story* supports this observation winsomely.

[5] Jeffrey Hadden was researching this mood on American campuses when this essay was written.

men" on their horizon are Safety, Success, Security, and Serenity. In the long view, this major segment of youth who are not "newsworthy" could pose a more serious threat to society than the noisy rebels and the earnest dissenters. Carbon copies of many in the old generation, they go along to get along, seek comfort above character, and honor convenience more than conscience. While an increasing number of youth do seek the basic reform of academe and the government, it is a minority who turn away from business and the professions as open highways to material success. Kenneth Keniston, Yale psychiatrist and informed observer of college youth, argues that this reform minority has its own silent majority.[6] That was certainly evident in the campus response to Cambodia, Kent State, and Jackson State. But will these moderates stick with the student reform movement or drift back into privatism? Presently, three quarters of the American students in 2,400 colleges and universities are not active reformers. They pose a greater threat to the humane society than their activist peers.

At the other end of the spectrum, less than one percent of the young people are bent on destroying America's social institutions. These few are nihilists, not reformers. They refuse to dialogue, cooperate, or compromise. They pose an immediate and frequently dangerous problem to the responsible administrator, the concerned policeman, the court judge, and the citizen on the streets—none of whom has the leisure or the freedom or the inclination or the raw courage to philosophize, dialogue, counsel, or befriend. The trial of "the Chicago Seven" burned that truth into America's consciousness. In dealing with this radical fringe, most adults at all levels tend to panic. Kingman Brewster of

[6] Kenneth Keniston, "Radicals Revisited," *Change in Higher Education I* (November-December, 1969), 25-33.

Yale—open, fair, firm, and honest with his student body and the New Haven assembly of Black Panthers—helped set the stage for peaceful demonstration and dialogue. The local police were equally responsible. This restrained, decent approach was more humane, and certainly more in keeping with American traditions, than the killing of several Panthers in Chicago in December, 1969.

We are not suggesting that it is easy to deal responsibly with convinced radicals. We are not implying that the law can be flaunted in or out of the courtroom. But we are saying that some radicals cannot get justice in many local courts today. We are saying that negative and harsh response to just criticisms of American society are immoral. We are saying that abusive language directed against the young and an arrogant indifference to their claims pushes moderates to be radicals and radicals to be revolutionaries. It is not enough "to lower our voices." The social crisis is too serious for that.

Perhaps twenty, certainly not more than thirty, percent of today's youth seriously desire reform and work *steadily* for it. This substantial minority (enlightened, concerned, independent) are the potential creators in tomorrow's society. If they are driven underground, alienated, crushed in spirit, America's single best national resource will be dissipated. These earnest dissenters and innovators must be given a place in our decision-making councils *now*. They are humanists who want our social institutions refashioned radically so that all human beings are not only free, but actively encouraged to become authentically human. They are supra-nationalists who want all people to live peacefully in a world where war is no longer accepted as diplomacy's ace-in-hole. They lack the "know-how" to achieve these humane (Christian) goals, but they have defined them, and that is a significant beginning. Public indifference, indiscriminate censure, disdain, and rejection only serve to incense and alienate them. These young radicals will not be put down. Their mounting recalcitrance is a significant socio-psychological-political strand in the fabric of contemporary society.[7] Events in the spring of 1970 supported that judgment.

On the 27th of April, 1970, *Time* reported that the Chicago Seven's Tom Hayden had advised a San Fernando Valley State College audience: "We turned out over a million people for the moratorium last fall, and the Establishment's response was to congratulate us because there was no violence. That wasn't the goal. The goal was to end the war. Demonstrations will not stay peaceful if the war in Vietnam doesn't end."[8] And they *were* ugly and harsh that week at Berkeley, Cambridge, New York City, and other places. The "shift from love to hate, from pacifism to violence" was frightening. A few days later President Nixon's announcement that American military forces had entered Cambodia had a triggering effect in the Kent State massacre and the general student strike which swept the nation. This time school administrators as well as professors joined the students. This time "moderate" students turned out by the tens of thousands to demonstrate peaceably. Significantly, many went beyond demonstration and set to work in and through the political, academic, and ecclesiastical Establishment for peace in southeast Asia. Signs of hope cropped up in unexpected places. Walter Hickel interceded publicly for the young people; Spiro Agnew omitted two pages of invective from an address in Idaho; government of-

[7] *Ibid.*
[8] *Time*, April 27, 1970, p. 27.

ficials gave thousands of hours to meetings with the student protesters; Nelson Rockefeller called college students of New York to elect representatives to a "permanent clearing house of ideas" that would provide a direct link to the governor's office; a bipartisan bloc of senators introduced an amendment to end the war in Vietnam by 1971; President Nixon, obviously shaken, assured the youth that he wanted peace in Vietnam. But who can predict what the situation will be by the time this capsule review of events in April-May, 1970, is published? It is likely that serious young people will escalate their criticisms of the state, church, and university.

Looking critically at the church, these realistic young people see little difference between the life style of church members and that of persons in other social organizations. Their sweeping judgment that ecclesiastical officials behave like ward politicians in spite of pious rhetoric, that pastors and priests are authoritarian or permissive, that lay leaders serve institutional ends like school administrators and corporation executives is not a massive caricature. Strip away the pious language and many churchmen (ordained and lay) are precisely what young people say they are, role-players. Meanwhile, increasing numbers of young people engage in serious theological conversations outside ecclesiastical boundaries. The institutional church, uncomfortable with nontheological and nonbiblical language, is psychologically unprepared to dialogue with them. Many of their questions and some of their affirmations are closer to the biblical tradition than the questions which most official church boards debate pompously or tediously at their monthly meetings. Socially concerned young people may be nearer to the God of the prophets than many middle-agers and oldsters who attend church for peace-of-mind homilies, organ preludes, and liturgical niceties.

Youth's frontal attack on education continues. Adults have been offended by their crass methods: "Up against the ivy wall, you. . . ." They have been frightened by the ugliness at Berkeley and Cambridge in late April 1970. The rebels are immature, unreasonable, and careless about the law. They are not shining saints; a few are demonic. But in most instances the academic community, like the government, drove them to open rebellion. To be specific: the Cox report on the Columbia revolt reveals that President Grayson Kirk, the trustees, and the faculty had declined to deal with student grievances and concerns in spite of repeated requests for dialogue and redressment. A report on student grievances at Columbia University had been gathering dust in President Kirk's files for seven months before the riots erupted. Too many professors in prestigious universities—whose critiques of government, church, and family life are insightful and sobering—have neglected to apply their talents at home. The human art of teaching has become an impersonal business in many universities. Only rarely does teaching facilitate learning among the students. Campus discontent on these and other counts is certainly legitimate.

When I attended college and graduate school, academic institutions determined the courses, credits, style of teaching (lecture), and grades; they also sought to dictate the life style of the students. The opportunities for learning in depth and for self-determination were limited. And there were rebellions in those days. Unfortunately, they were spurious, prankish, ineffective. By the 1960's, student rebellions had become sustained attacks on the nondemocracy which has characterized the college-university since its establishment on American shores in 1636. Today's student activists have achieved results because their disruptive methods forced paternalistic and arbitrary university administrations to face reality. The young people, like black militants, have concluded that the wheel that squeaks the loudest gets the grease in a bureaucratic society.

Comparatively few people have access to the "corridors of power" in our culture. Consequently, the majority, seeking to get their views heard, turn to the only media open to them: letters to the local editor, complaints to the municipal administrators, and the use of local, state, and national ballots. When these media prove to be ineffective for these citizens, they are forced to protest, demonstrate, riot. This is not new. Student rebellions closed Harvard for a season in colonial days; they sparked the liberal revolutions in Europe in 1830 and 1848; they rocked Paris in 1968. Two hundred years ago America's Founding Fathers declared in cold print that, when it became evident the members of Parliament had refused to grant them representation, it was England, not they, who had precipitated the rebellion. Unless middle-agers and senior citizens flexibilize their thinking and foster creative social changes now, a larger revolution than the one begun in 1775 could engulf this nation before the century is over.

Finally, we reassert youth's disillusionment with their government. Vigorous and violent dissent from governmental policies is not a new strand in American history. But the fact that young people are now in the forefront of the political dissenters *is* new. The democratization of American society has been a messy process of dissent, confrontation, and occasional rebellion. Disorder has been a strand in American history since the days of Bacon's Rebellion (farmers) against the landed aristocracy in colonial Virginia in 1676. A dominant factor in the settlement of American shores was the colonizers' dissent from and rebellion against the home government and/or the home church in Europe. "Discontented and mutinous speeches" filled the cabin of the *Mayflower*; some Pilgrims threatened to "use their own liberty." John Smith presided over a "police state" to keep Jamestown on the map. Since 1607 and 1620, the course of American history has been disruptive. But Rap Brown is inaccurate in his declaration that violence is "as American as apple pie." Violence is as human as apple pie is American. Violence is a continuing strand in *human* history—from Cain and Herod to Bull Connor and Eldridge Cleaver. No nation or race has a corner on it. Dissent is as American as apple pie. The genius of the American political system has been that it has adapted to the pressures of changing socio-economic situations. The system failed only once, 1861–1865.

Certainly dissent in America is not dead. Youthful critics of the Vietnam war contributed substantially to the decision of President Johnson to step down. A segment of America's youth are not insensitive to moral issues or disdainful of engaging in political action. When Senator Eugene McCarthy opposed President Johnson on the Vietnam war young people flocked to his banner so eagerly that the campaign was dubbed "The Children's Crusade." Youth were also attracted strongly to Robert Kennedy. His compassion for the dispossessed, his bold confession of error on the Vietnam War, and his openness to social change "turned on" millions of young people. Robert Kennedy's assassination dashed their hopes.[9] Both McCarthy and

[9] See Jack Newfield, *Robert Kennedy: A Memoir* (New York: E. P. Dutton, 1969).

Kennedy were "over thirty," yet they captivated young people by their candor, imagination, and political existentialism. In May, 1970, McGovern, Church, Goodell, Hatfield, Hickel, Muskie, Hughes, and others were proving that they could communicate with youth, too. And the young people began to work again with the political Establishment as they had from 1960 to 1968. The generation gap can be bridged in our political society.

But the current social situation in this nation remains critical. A substantial bloc of youth and other militant minorities are attacking all our social institutions because they are critical of the values and goals of our society. The widening gap between generations (and races and classes) will not be bridged until responsible adults meet the young radicals honestly on real issues: war and peace, race, poverty, materialism. Young people are right when they argue that every individual has the right to be free to become a person instead of cannon fodder for the state, a number in the university, a cog in the corporation. Young people are right when they insist that the church prove the relevance of its message in the urban ghettoes, the deserts of poverty, and the inner world of the family. Young people are right when they demand imagination and a concern for persons in those who wield power in the local, state, and national political institutions. But adults are also right when they point to a "tangled world," to the ambiguities of history, to the tragic strand in life. Adults are right when they argue that nothing worthwhile is "instant." Candor, imagination, and temper of mind, more than chronology, divide the generations.

What then can be done immediately to bridge the communication, credibility, expectation, and performance gaps among three generations?

## IV

First, persons in each generation can strive for openness, sensitivity, and objectivity in seeking jointly to identify and address those social-economic-political forces which dehumanize society. In this, a firm word needs to be said to a segment of young people (white and black) who assume arrogantly that all adults are out of touch with reality, and to a larger segment of adults who simply refuse to listen to their tortured young. There are youth who are more mature emotionally than many adults; conversely, some adults are more imaginative and open that many young people. The "now generation" has no corner on "telling it like it is"; the generation in power is not all-wise. Humility is a quality that must be cultivated by all human beings.

Second, persons in each generation can strive diligently to provide seasons of privacy in all human relationships. There is a psychological limit to truth-telling. Candid criticism and bold confrontation can be overdone. Husbands and wives and children, especially teenagers, need seasons of privacy. This need is positively crucial in parent-teen relationships. During the years when I served first as a professor at Gettysburg College and later as pastor of the College Church there, scores of parents asked (and pressured) me to persuade their sons and daughters to choose professions which had parental approval. In some cases, parents had so conditioned their children to the rightness of a particular profession or vocation that when these inquisitive young people examined another vocation they experienced guilt. Today, the tables are turned. Some young people precipitate guilt in their parents by disdaining their parents' professions and vocations. A young man working for a Ph.D. in the humanities, his education financed by his father, is less than human if he despises his father's business (profession) and money which provide the means for that education in the humanities. Truth enlightens and heals only when it is spoken with compassion and appreciation for one's own and another's historical situation. Criticism, however honest and relevant, is rarely constructive if it is self-righteous. Anger can motivate positively if it is employed in the context of acceptance, tolerance, and compassion.

Third, persons in each generation can strive to bring freedom and discipline into personal and social equilibrium. Freedom without discipline ends in anarchy; discipline without freedom ends in tyranny. In either case humanity is despoiled. This issue is intensely complex for "what one man calls justice, another calls expropriation; and one man's security is another man's slavery; and one man's liberty is another's anarchy." [10] But the stakes have become too high for any citizen to "cop out." Polarization between the permissive society and the coercive society, between self-righteous dissenters and self-righteous "law-and-order" advocates, between militant blacks and reactionary whites, between arrogant youth and insensitive adults threatens to smash the institutions of contemporary society.

Finally, there is need for charity (love, *agape*) between the generations. Accusations, recriminations, antagonism, hostility, and alienation are shattering trust, mutilating persons, and tearing society to pieces. It is not enough "to lower our voices." It is not enough to provide relevant critiques and brilliant analyses. Presently, there is pressing need to heal personal wounds and social ruptures. That need is as urgent now as it

[10] Milton Mayer, *On Liberty: Man v. The State* (Santa Barbara: The Center for the Study of Democratic Institutions, 1969), p. 41.

was at the close of the Civil War. Lincoln's plea for truth and charity is as relevant today as it was on the 4th of March, 1865. Ian McLaren, looking back on a creative ministry in his native Scotland, declared flatly that if he had it to do all over again he would be more kind. Healing between and among the generations (and races, classes, religionists, and political ideologies) is an imperative if society is to become whole. Youth's plea, "Make love, not war," is absurdly simplistic in the face of history's ambiguities, but it is elementally sound. Every home and every social group needs a Desdemona: "She is so free, so kind, so apt, so blessed a disposition, she holds it a vice in her goodness not to do more than is requested." [11]

The generation gap occurs every several decades. In 1971, the gap is *qualitatively* different from the gap between generations in other eras of history. But the breach can be bridged. A common point at which the generations can begin is for them to adapt all their allegiances to a commitment to truth and a concern for persons. That is especially essential for citizens in the sovereign state (democratic or totalitarian) in this revolutionary era. The superpatriot and the anarchist are equally destructive. We shall take some soundings on this deep issue in the next chapter.

[11] Shakespeare's *Othello*.

Charles Townshend: "*Will these Americans, children planted by our care, nourished up by our indulgence until they are grown to a degree of strength and opulence, and protected by our arms, will they grudge to contribute their mite to relieve us from the heavy weight of that burden which we live under?*"

Colonel Isaac Barré: "*They planted by your care?* No! *Your oppressions planted 'em in America. They fled your tyranny to a then uncultivated and inhospitable country where they exposed themselves to almost all the hardships to which human nature is liable, and among others to the cruelties of a savage foe. . . .*

"*They nourished by your indulgence? They grew by your neglect of 'em, As soon as you began to care about 'em, that care was exercised in sending persons to rule over 'em. . . .*

"*They protected by your arms? They have nobly taken up arms in your defence, have exerted a valour amidst their constant and laborious industry for the defence of a country, whose frontier while drenched in blood, its interior parts have yielded all its little savings to your emolument. And believe me, remember I this day told you so, that same spirit of freedom which activated that people at first, will accompany them still.*"

From the debate in the House of Commons on the Stamp Act, 1765. Quoted in Merrill D. Peterson, *Thomas Jefferson and the New Nation* (New York: Oxford University Press, 1970), p. 32.

# IV

# CAN ONE BE CHRISTIAN AND PATRIOTIC AT THE SAME TIME?

Serious churchmen engage in a continuing examination of the relationship between Christ and culture. H. Richard Niebuhr called this essential activity "the double wrestle of the church with its Lord and with the cultural society with which it lives. . . ."[1] Responsible citizens also examine critically the relationship between the church and the state. These complex, interrelated issues are especially relevant in today's world of 130 competing sovereign states, colliding cultures and subcultures, and a half dozen regionally influential religions that call their adherents to interpretations of God, man, and society which are in conflict with one another.

This essay on these crucial issues attempts to point up several salient concerns for the Christian church in Western society: (1) its need to free itself from simplistic views on the ambivalent relationship between Christ and culture, and on the overt and covert interactions between church and state; (2) the need to encourage its members and all citizens to view politics as one viable means for creating a humane society; (3) the need to prod its members and all citizens to bring factual knowledge, insight, understanding, and integrity to political decision-making in a society which is both free and totalitarian; (4) the need to accept human freedom as a dreadful gift; and (5) the need to recognize that God is at work in the ambiguities and tragedies of history.

[1] *Christ and Culture* (New York: Harper & Row, 1951), p. 3.

Consequently, we shall review the historical perspective on the emergence of sovereign states, examine the messiness of political decision-making in nations with subcultures, and sketch the classical views on "Christ and Culture" before we tackle the practical question posed in this chapter.

## *HISTORICAL PERSPECTIVE*

The twentieth-century constellation of sovereign states in Europe took shape three hundred years ago in Western Europe. For millenia tribal relationships had been the bench marks of man's social experience. Late in the history of man, Rome brought the sovereign state to effective actuality. When Rome collapsed in the fifth century A.D., tribal relationships again became dominant. Except for a brief moment under Charlemagne in the early Middle Ages (ninth century), Angles, Saxons, Franks, Jutes, Vikings, Bohemians, Slavs, Poles, Magyars, Tartars, and a host of other ethnic tribes fought locally and regionally. Here and there (Norman Conquest), regional amalgamations occurred, but there were no sovereign nation-states. The high Middle Ages produced feudal society presided over by warring kings who were powerful lords. The closing Middle Ages, having produced the commercial city-states in Italy and Germany, provided the dynamics for the sovereign state.

As a matter of historical record, sovereign states emerged firmly during the sixteenth and seventeenth centuries: Spain (Ferdinand and Isabella), the Dutch Netherlands, England (the Tudors), France (the Bourbons), and Russia (Peter and Catherine). These sovereign political-states were shaped in response to the economic, social, religious, and military dynamics of the revolutionary sixteenth and seventeenth centuries.

In the eighteenth century, the American and the French Revolutions turned the sovereign political-state into the sovereign nation-state (flag, anthem, citizen army, patriotism). Bismarck and Cavour applied their Machiavellian skills to nation building through carefully cultivated wars. The United States achieved full political sovereignty in the blood and exhaustion (South) of civil war (1861–65) and proceeded, especially in the twentieth century, to become a gigantic world power. Likewise, Russia, resuming her four-hundred-years' struggle to overcome the national devastation done by the Mongols, claimed a dominant place in the world community of nations during 1917–45. Japan, China, and national states in Africa, Asia, and Latin America followed suit, 1920–70. Each of these nation states centers in a particular government supported by millions of citizens who give their primary loyalty, voluntarily or involuntarily, to "their" nation. By one means or another, each national government commands the primary loyalty of a majority of its citizens. Each citizen-nation-state, a phenomenon of modern times, complicates relations between itself and other sovereign states in economic, territorial, religious, and ideological competition with one another.

How does this dynamic phenomenon of modern culture affect one's view of Christ? How does man's understanding of the gospel affect his cultural relationships in general and his relationships with the sovereign state in particular? To what degree does the nation-state influence human life? Is it possible for a citizen to be earnestly Christian and responsibly patriotic at the same time in America or Russia, England or China in 1971?

The complex nature of these questions inundates simplistic answers. In elemental terms the issue requires us to recognize that every individual has his own concept of Christianity and culture, each manages his own existential mix of faith, culture, and patriotism. Both culture and personal faith affect how each citizen thinks and feels and acts. It is religious persuasion, for example. which gives the Quaker his indisposition toward the state's military service. On the other hand, "the consent of the governed"—a meaningful political concept to people in Western Europe, the United States, and Canada—influences their citizenry in varying degrees. But the concept is empty for the peoples of Asia and most in the Third World.

## *SUBCULTURES IN COLLISION*

Consequently, serious Christians must set out to discover what they really think about the gospel in the context of their culture and in relation to other cultures. This tangled task is complicated further by the subculture in which one lives. The United States, for example, is the beneficiary of and contributor to Western culture. But American culture is markedly different from French or German culture. The English, Irish, Welsh, and Scots comprise Great Britain, but each has a different culture. A striking illustration of this conflict of loyalties is the story that went the rounds in Ireland during the Black and Tan guerilla warfare against the English. An Irishman confessed to his priest that he had killed Englishmen: "Ah yes," the confessor responded, "but have you no sins to confess?" Religion is still a factor in the presently troubled Irish State. Communists and churchmen collide not only in Czechoslovakia but also in France and Italy.

In the United States, the residents of New York City differ culturally from their fellow citizens in Biloxi, Mississippi. The subculture in Southern California is different from the subculture in Indiana. Some Main Line Philadelphians are more comfortable in Kensington, London, than in Los Angeles, California. Jacob Javits, senior Senator from New York, could not have been nominated in Alabama. These wide differences in subcultures have a marked influence on the churches in different sections of the United States. During the nineteenth century the collision course between two subcultures with conflicting economic goals, social purposes, and political ideologies ended violently in America's "Civil War." The churches also divided —North and South.

There has never been a decade in American history when subcultural tensions have not seethed behind the facade of national "unity." Occasionally, they have broken into the open (the Whiskey Rebellion, the New England Confederation, South Carolina's Nullification Acts, the farmers, laborers, blacks, youth, etc). One current aspect of deep-seated conflict came into plain view when George Wallace won the presidential electors of Georgia, Alabama, Mississippi, Louisiana, and Arkansas and captured substantial segments of the political constituencies of Florida, South Carolina, North Carolina, Tennessee, Kentucky, and Viriginia in the national election of 1968. Wallace's 1970 nomination for the governorship in Alabama keeps sectionalism alive. Current efforts to rebuild the Republican Party by exploiting sectional (subcultural) differences in American society are risky indeed.

At the same time, we must keep firmly in mind that the forces which hold America together are complex, vigorous, and deep.[2] It is historically unrealistic and politically ineffective to ignore this reality.

[2] See Daniel Boorstin's *The Decline of Radicalism* (New York: The Macmillan Co., 1968).

## *DIFFERING VIEWS ON CHRIST AND CULTURE* [3]

Next, we shall sketch the classical views on Christ and culture, church and state. Each view has its adherents in contemporary American society.

One view places Christ above culture. From the first generation of Christians to today's generation in America, this view has had strong supporters. The argument is that Christ is outside of, above, unrelated to culture. God is concerned only with man's "spiritual life." The gospel is not related to his worldly concerns: social, political, economic. Christianity is a private affair; the church has no business speaking to public issues. This view has had triumphant seasons in the calendar of Christian history, and there are evidences of its continuing vitality in contemporary society.

Monasticism (fostered vigorously by the medieval church and supported by the hierarchal society of feudalism) is still a social option in our world community. Attacks on it are mounting in Catholic circles; but monasticism remains a psycho-social-religious force in many quarters of society today. But the notion that man can withdraw from the world, keep himself pure by abstaining from direct involvement in society, and live congenially with Jesus (or truth) has no precedent in biblical Christianity. A product of culture and human nature, it is not always formally religious: the "ivory-tower" professor, the "pure" scientist, the isolated political leader, and Bob Dylan singing a completely "personal" salvation. One segment of youth, we observed in chapter III, is devoted to "privatism"; its adherents seek an escape from worldly pressures.

Another example of Christ above culture is sectarian Christianity. During the seventeenth century, bands of

[3] I am indebted to H. Richard Niebuhr for this summary statement.

committed Christians, persecuted during and impoverished by the religious wars in Europe, established communal life apart from the "evil" society which afflicted them. The sincerity of most sectarians (and monastics) is above reproach, but their major premise is not biblical. It roots in culture and human nature. No one can place Christ outside his own historical experience without losing his personal relationship with Christ as he is.[4] The judgment that Christ and culture can be separated is unrealistic, for God is active in his world. Further, sectarianism does not free its adherents from basic political responsibilities in the sovereign state. Sectarian Christians discover that the state requires them to pay taxes too. The sectarian's conscientious objection to war is honored by the United States government, but exemption from military service is a privilege granted by the state; it is not a personal right guaranteed by law. The exemption can be cancelled anytime the government decides to do so. If that were to occur, it is likely that many members in the "peace churches" would suffer imprisonment rather than accept active service in the military, but that is not the issue in this discussion.

However, the view that Christ is unrelated to culture is not limited to monastics and sectarians. It is firmly entertained by millions of main-line Protestant, Catholic, and Orthodox churchmen. They too are convinced that the church should not talk about politics or economics. Religion is a private affair. On the other hand, many twentieth-century laymen in Europe and America agree with Lord Melbourne who, on leaving a church where a revival meeting was underway, exclaimed angrily that "things have come to a pretty pass

[4] See Niebuhr, *The Responsible Self,* chapter 2.

when religion is made to invade the sphere of private life." In the grass roots church, many people resent Christianity's "invasion" of private life (stewardship of money, personal witness, sexual activities) more intensely than those who object to its "invasion" of public life. But the biblical view calls the church to bring both private and public life under the Word of God for the sake of humanity. That is one clear implication of the Incarnation. To deny that implication is to emasculate biblical Christianity. Jesus was not a disembodied spirit. He lived in the world under the legal jurisdiction of Rome. And he died at the hands of a Roman governor.

Another view on Christ and culture represents the opposite end of the spectrum: culture above Christ. That was the inflexible position of Imperial Rome: "Hail, Caesar, we who are about to die salute you." The one honest political charge brought against Jesus was that he put God above the Roman Emperor (the state). And he did precisely that. From the sovereign state's point of view he was not only a dissenter, he was also a rebel. This view has contemporary overtones. Mussolini maneuvered his Fascist Party into a position of power over the Catholic Church in Italy during the 1920's and 1930's. The Nazi state domesticated the church. The institutional church in Soviet Russia and its satellite states has a tenuous existence only because it is a subservient church. It is well attested that there was and is a Christian remnant in the church in the totalitarian states of the twentieth century, but that is not the issue here. Joseph Hromadka's heartbroken letter to the Kremlin after the Soviets' 1968 purge of Czechoslovakia's liberal political leadership puts the basic issue in clear perspective: the totalitarian state cannot and will not tolerate *any* free social institution which is critical of its political deeds. The recognition of this hard reality is not equivalent to the political rightists' erroneous assumption that the "Communists" are behind every door in the government, the church, and the university in the United States.

But millions of comfortable Americans who criticize the Communists' oppressive political measures against dissenting churchmen, educators, editors, scientists, poets, and novelists proceed (in a lesser degree) to support an Establishment press, foster public education which is subservient to political necessities, endorse a federal government which clings neurotically to the status quo, and criticize a church which is actively concerned for persons-in-society. Most American church members are culturally controlled rather than Christ-oriented in making and spending their money, choosing a vocation, and achieving their social aims. They honor the state above the church in pursuing political goals and national interests. There is strong evidence that the Christian ethic is to them an inconvenience, an embarrassment, a liability. Some admit that readily; others deny it self-righteously. Christ is not widely acknowledged as Lord of the church or of any other social institution in American society. The cultural accommodationists dominate the Christian church in America. Conflict is inevitable when churchmen like King, Groppi, Berrigan, and Stringfellow come on the scene. Tensions develop in the church and the community when it speaks on war and peace, housing, education, welfare, or sex.

A third view of Christ and culture is syncretistic. This view calls for the gospel and culture to be a meld. Some scholars judge that an almost perfect meld occurred during the high Middle Ages, the so-called "Age of Faith." Other scholars disagree. In spite of the medieval scholars' squabble over "who's on first, who's on second," the syncretistic view did reach its high-water mark during the thirteenth century when Thomas Aquinas (just price, etc.) was the dominant figure in Western thought. Rational reductions were made in the ethic of Jesus; the secular ethic was upgraded.

Presently, this appears to be the condition of contemporary American Christianity and culture. But Christian syncretism is not a phenomenon of the thirteenth and twentieth centuries; it has a long history. In the eighth century B.C. the Hebrew prophets—Amos, Isaiah, Hosea, and Micah—attacked it relentlessly. Jesus pointed up its dangers. Paul railed against it. The disturbing truth for American Christians is that biblical religion is not syncretistic yet they have made it that.

A fourth view contends that Christianity and culture exist in tension: the Christian must decide personal and social issues daily in the light of Christ's mind in him and pay the price for doing so. This was Paul's view. He exhorted the little bands of Christians to honor the state. But he insisted that honor be given without their allowing the world to squeeze them into its mold. Augustine and Luther took over the Pauline view. Augustine made it conversionist. Luther fashioned it into "the doctrine of the two Kingdoms." Handled flexibly, related dynamically to modern society, and formulated in today's idiom, both variants offer clues for living responsibly under the gospel in the sovereign state.

But we must also keep in mind that Christianity is supra-national. The issue is not only "church and state"; it is equally "church and states."

The trouble with most church-state doctrines is that they are purely domesticated in trying to locate Christianity somewhere within the state. Whether or not the legal doctrine of national sovereignty is made explicit, there is an assumption that the nation-state defines the outer boundaries of Christian concern and influence. This is both ethically cramped and historically short-sighted. The state is not the largest arena within which the church exists: the church has a trans-national life which touches a vast plurality of states. This whole realm of ethical and legal discussion would be better identified as "church-and-states." [5]

Augustine's classical image of the City of God and the city of man, and Luther's dynamic concept of Two Kingdoms combine to offer new light on the tensions which arise today in man's ethical and political decision-making at home and across national boundaries. Americans are ethically obligated by *their* Constitution to respect Buddhists in Vietnam, Hindus in India, and Moslems in the Arab states. Christians in all nations are morally obligated by the Cross to engage in Christian dialogues with all people, including Marxists.[6]

The Apostolic Faith existed for three centuries as an illegal religion and spread through the Mediterranean world. Early in the fourth century Constantine legalized Christianity. That event created a new historical situation for the church. Its membership soared; its institutional forms mushroomed; it became a landowner; it pursued power. By the eleventh century the ecclesiastical institution in the West was so ambitious for secular power that it came within a shade of bringing the state under its domination (Henry IV at Canossa). Five centuries later the Calvinists, a vigorous segment in the Reformation, made a similar power-grab by establishing a theocratic government in Geneva.

[5] Alan Geyer, *Piety and Politics* (Richmond: John Knox Press, 1963).

[6] See Jan Milič Lochman, *Church in a Marxist Society* (New York: Harper & Row, 1970).

Its secular power was demonstrated appallingly when Michael Servetus, a dissenter from Calvinism, was executed. A century later in colonial New England, the Puritans defined private morality through political legislation.

Paul did not endorse this view. Rejecting monasticism, sectarianism, and syncretism, he laid the foundation for the doctrine of "The Two Kingdoms": Christ and culture, church and state, exist in tension. The Christian has obligations to both, but his final allegiance in any conflict which *he* perceives between the two belongs to God. His active witness may or may not convert the secular (state) mind, but the Christian is obligated to make it or become less than human (Christian). The best chance to transform society rests with Christians who not only employ political media to create a humane society, but also dissent from and resist State policies and deeds which dehumanize society.

Thomas Jefferson, brooding over the reenactment of the religious persecutions of Europe on American shores, arrived at the Pauline view pragmatically. Having authored the Statute of Religious Freedom in Virginia, Mr. Jefferson insisted on an amendment to the Federal Constitution which provided for the separation of church and state as distinct and necessary institutions of society. Like Paul, Jefferson also recognized, accepted, supported, and fostered the view that churchmen, also citizens, would speak to political and social issues.[7]

Contemporary American church members are not

[7] Any serious effort to understand American politics requires that one explore the mind of Thomas Jefferson. The best work on Jefferson's formative influence upon American democracy is Merrill D. Peterson, *Thomas Jefferson and the New Nation* (New York: Oxford University Press, 1970).

realistic about their political and biblical traditions. Every Christian's attitude toward politics and economics and other social issues inevitably reflects his emotional and intellectual commitment to Christ, or lack of it. How could it be otherwise? Christians are also citizens. The fundamentalist who argues that the church should "preach Christ" and stay out of politics can be vociferous himself on the issue of Bible reading and prayer in the public schools! He is political when his *religious* views are at stake. Because it usually depends on whose ox is being gored, the constitutional separation of church and state is pragmatically ingenious. It guarantees that the state cannot dictate what the church's witness shall be. Equally, it guarantees that a sect or denomination or the whole of Christendom cannot dictate that the state legislate in favor of a particular sect or denomination or Christendom itself. The Mormon Church or the Catholic Church cannot require the Federal government to legislate either's view of marriage. Jefferson and his contemporaries, like Paul, Luther, and Calvin before them, would be distressed by the shallow moralism of contemporary churchmen who insist that the church has no right to speak on political issues which affect all society—war, poverty, racism, ecology. Only if the church denies the Incarnation can it remain silent.

Interaction between the institutions of church and state is inevitable because church members are citizens of the state. The separation of the institutions of church and state safeguards non-church citizens and churchmen-citizens against coercive measures initiated and pursued by either institution. In countries where a state church did exist or exists now, religious minorities have been or are discriminated against: the Huguenots in France, the Anabaptists in Germany, the

Puritans in England, the Quakers in New England, the Hindus and Moslems in India and Pakistan, the Buddhists in Vietnam, etc. Both Spain and Latin America were severely maimed by ecclesiastical meddling in their political life until recently. "The Catholic Church has been at the heart of political controversy throughout most of Latin America's history, and this conflict has left it weak. Until the nineteenth century, the church was an arm not only of the Spanish Conquest but of the colonial government as well. . . ."[8] Presently, however, in Brazil "the Roman Catholic hierarchy is engaged with the six-year-old military dictatorship in the gravest church-state conflict of the hemsiphere."[9] Whether the Roman Catholic Church will continue in its newfound concern for social justice in an unjust society or retrench behind traditional forms which stultify faith is the agony of Catholicism throughout Latin America today. If Catholicism is true to its prophetic role, political and religious polarization will be acute in the southern hemisphere. If it retrenches, Catholicism may die in Latin America.

The cleavage is not yet that deep in Catholic, Protestant, and Orthodox churches in the United States; but it is deepening. While the institutions of church and state remain separate in North America, they do interact on each other through their human constituencies. A survey of American history reveals that churchmen joined actively with nonchurchmen in building the American political society on the foundations of England's Atlantic community.[10] To give a specific example: at College Church in Gettysburg,

[8] Norman Gall, "Latin America: The Church Militant," *Commentary* XLIX (April, 1970), 26 and 28.

[9] *Ibid.*

[10] Sydney Mead, *The Lively Experiment* (New York: Harper & Row, 1967), chapters 1 and 2.

Pennsylvania, a nineteenth-century Lutheran theologian, ecumenist, and scholar, Professor Samuel S. Smucker, preached hour-long sermons against the Mexican War in 1846 and against slavery in the 1850's. In those days the members of the congregation agreed and disagreed with the sermonic thrusts, but they did not argue that the church should be silent on those political issues. Unfortunately, that brand of realism evaporated in the church after World War I. During 1930–48, the socially conscious pastor in College Church, Doctor Dwight F. Putman, fought doggedly to reclaim the pulpit's right to speak on social and political issues. During 1952–54, Doctor Putman's successor at College Church, then serving in historic Trinity Church, Lancaster, Pennsylvania (1729), had to cut through layers of human piety there to bring Joseph McCarthy's diabolical deeds (eg., political assassination by association) under the judgment of God and human law.

In most places during this century the church in America has moved backward in addressing social issues. This massive flight from political responsibility is not biblical; it is not constitutional; it is not realistic. Practical politics and Christian piety cannot be compartmentalized. Our forebears recognized, accepted, and honored that reality. Contemporary churchmen need to re-examine—on biblical, theological, constitutional, sociological, and psychological grounds—the relations between church and state. They must also examine carefully the relationship between Christ and culture, if they expect to be honest Christians and responsible citizens.

## *FAITH AND PATRIOTISM*

Now, we can inquire: "Is it possible for one to be Christian and patriotic at the same time?" More light than heat will be shed on this question if we define what we mean by "Christian" and by "patriotic." All human beings tend to use words to communicate their personal convictions, theories, and prejudices. Consequently words can be misleading. Used carelessly or deviously, words become meaningless. Integrity and common sense require that we define the meanings we attach to the words "Christian" and "patriotic" in this presentation.

First, the word "Christian." Biblical theology corrects denominational, sectarian, and cultural views on what it means to be Christian. For example, a Christian is described simply in the Book of Acts as a follower of the Way (Jesus). Historically, the word "Christian" derives from the once treasonable charge, "Christ-follower." That too is a corrective. From Augustine (fourth century) to the eve of the Reformation (sixteenth century), a "Christian" was identified as one who accepted the official teachings of the church and its authority. Dissent was heresy, and heretics were punished. So, Joan of Arc and John Hus were burned at the stake; Henry VIII was excommunicated. Then the Reformation provided a radically different definition of the "Christian" as one who searches the scripture for himself, honors his conscience when it is captive to the Word of God, and acts boldly on his Christian insights. Some devotees of the Reformation (sectarian) pressed this to a subjective conclusion: the Divine Light within is one's final authority. So, rigidity returned. In Oliver Cromwell's England and Cotton Mather's New England the "Christian" was one who subscribed to the tenets of Puritanism; Catholics and Quakers were heretics. A current definition of the word "Christian" owes its origin to Dietrich Bonhoeffer: "the man for others." He described the "Christian" in terms of the ethical decisions he makes in historical situations. Each of these descriptions has a measure of truth. None, however, incorporates the essential biblical description of the Christian.

Our definition of "Christian" is framed essentially from the prophets and the apostles. Consequently, it does not focus on morality or doctrine or ethics or worldly involvement. It focuses on the relationship between persons.[11] A "Christian" is a person, created by God in his own likeness (person), who is free to live in an ever-changing relationship with the Person, Jesus Christ. This personal relationship is not static, but dynamic. Maintained in freedom, the relationship is the source of the Christian person's moral character, ethical decisions, doctrinal descriptions, and worldly involvement. This definition rests on God's deed in Christ and on human freedom. It disavows all efforts to define God and man statically. It emphasizes the Christian's freedom to relate to God and to other persons as he wills. Dostoevsky caught the essence of this voluntary relationship when he caused the Grand Inquisitor to say to the Prisoner (Christ): "In place of the rigid ancient law, man must hereafter with free heart decide for himself what is good and what is evil, having only Thy image before him as his guide." [12] Broadly, this is the sense in which we use the word, "Christian."

Next, the word "patriot." Here it is difficult to frame a meaningful definition because there is no authoritative source (scripture in the church) which provides a norm for judgment. But if we accept history as a reasonable description of persons-and-events-in-society, we have a relatively "objective" frame of reference for

[11] Specifically, I am indebted to Charles M. Jacobs, *What, Then Is Christianity?* (Philadelphia: Fortress Press, 1940).

[12] *The Brothers Karamazov* (New York: Modern Library), p. 264.

our attempt to fashion a working definition. Webster's unabridged dictionary offers a score of different meanings. Among them are these. (1) A "patriot" is one who loves and defends his country and works for its immediate and long-range interests. (2) A "patriot" is one who advocates, promotes, and fights for the independence of his country from another country or group of nations (self-determination). Under the first definition, Senator McGovern can be identified as a patriot because he works for America's disengagement from the Vietnam War—an objective which he and millions more consider to be in the best interests of this country and humanity. Employing the second definition, George Washington, who fought for the Colonies' independence from Britain, can be identified as a patriot. But if we employ *this* definition in judging our political contemporaries, we must conclude that black and yellow leaders, seeking the independence of their countries in Africa and Asia from one-time colonial powers, are patriots. We Americans hallow our Revolutionary forefathers as patriots. We forget that George III and his ministers branded them as rebels. Latin Americans view Castro, Africans view Nasser, and Asians view Mao as patriots. Many Americans label all three as revolutionaries.

Obviously, the second definition is not precise enough for Americans. Indeed, it may be useless anywhere in this revolutionary age. We shall use the first definition: a "patriot" is one who loves his country, defends it in the event of direct attack if its government serves persons (living in Nazi Germany he would have refused to support the state), and promotes its interests so long as they are humane (he dissents vigorously against the Vietnam war). In this context, we judge that the advocates of the Confederacy in the

1850's were not patriots. Southern leadership, holding rigidly to a doctrine of state's rights, promoted economic and social and cultural aims which benefited the plantation owners, depressed the poor whites, kept the blacks in bondage, disrupted the nation, and laid waste to the South. If a patriot is one who rises above his personal desires and natural bent to secure advantages for his region at the expense of other regions, and who actively advocates policies which will benefit the greatest number of people in his nation and in other nations, then George Wallace and those who supported him in 1968 and in 1970, are scarcely true patriots. It is obvious that they are not dedicated to the best interests of the whole nation. On the other hand, the handful of black anarchists, bent on destroying everything unless they get their way at once, are not patriots. Like the blue collar workers of Mississippi, they are less sensitive to others' needs than to their own. If rapid disengagement from the Vietnam War is in the best interests of this nation, as millions consider it to be, then those youth who participated in the several peace moratoria are patriots. To the extent that President Nixon actually disengages our forces from Indo-China, as he has promised to do, he is a patriot even though his methods differ from Senator McGovern's. If the white majority accepts the principle that whatever benefits twenty million blacks will strengthen this national state and secure a base for peace and act on it, they are patriots. Many citizens, black and white, need to develop an objective frame of reference for tolerance and dissent in the United States.

Allowing for differences in style, which human freedom spawns, one can be Christian and patriotic at the same time in the context in which we have defined the words. But tension is always there; and in many situations conflict is inevitable.[13] Whether it will be creative depends on those who seek not peace at any price, but honest political compromise and Christian reconciliation.

Having arrived at a situational position for suggesting an answer to our question, we turn finally to the tribunal of biblical evidence to discern what Jesus had to say on this question. In the progressive revelation of God (recorded in the scriptures), there is an uneven but maturing concept of man's primary relationship with God and with his fellow men. In the early history of the Hebrews, loyalty to God and his people, the nation, were identical. First and Second Kings and First and Second Chronicles incorporate this view substantially: the Lord of Hosts helps the Israelites triumph over their enemies. Yet even these crude provincial stories suggest that God helps only those who are loyal to him. Joshua, for example, opposed a nationalistic war because God disapproved of it. The prophets of the eighth century refined and enlarged this view; they saw God above their nation, judging it for disloyalty to him and devotion to its own selfish purposes. Jeremiah's use of God's plumb-line is a case in point. Jesus expanded the prophetic vision to universal proportions: God invites and requires a loyalty which transcends not only the nation but also race, color, sex, generations *and* creeds. He defined His community as supra-national.

But Jesus' teaching offended the narrow religious interests of the Pharisees. Eventually, it also jarred the sovereign claims of Rome so that the state authorized his crucifixion. The Pharisees, getting this issue into the

[13] See Geyer, *Piety and Politics*, pp. 58-102; and O. Fred Nolde, *The Churches and the Nations* (Philadelphia: Fortress Press, 1970); James Finn, ed., *A Conflict of Loyalties: The Case for Selective Conscientious Objection* (New York: Pegasus, 1968); and William O. Douglas, *Points of Rebellion* (New York: Vintage Books, 1970).

open, asked: Should one give primary allegiance to Caesar since Rome ruled Judea or should one give his basic loyalty to God? Jesus responded by asking for a coin of the realm and inquiring whose inscription was on it. His adversaries answered, "Caesar's." Jesus' counsel was elemental and intellectually honest: "Render to Caesar the things that are Caesar's and to God the things that are God's."

Jesus went to the heart of the issue; each person must discover for himself which loyalty is which in life's constantly changing political and social situations. God is not totalitarian; he lets man free to decide his own allegiances. But Jesus made it plain that one has obligations to the state as well as to God. Each must discern those obligations for himself and act on them. The "Christian" who consistently seeks to avoid all social and political responsibilities is neither Christian nor patriotic in the biblical sense, nor is the political absolutist or the syncretist religious.

But how does one discern in any particular moment of history what belongs to the state and what belongs to God? Simon Peter, proclaiming Christ in an antagonistic Roman culture and a hostile Jewish society, set it down that Christians are called to obey God rather than men. That means that a directive from any individual, private association, ecclesiastical or political society which requires one to speak or act contrary to his conscience will find the Christian honoring God, that is dissenting from and resisting the human directive. But no one can determine what violates the conscience of another, and no one is entitled to that prerogative. God himself does not assume it. For Simon Peter and hundreds more in the first several centuries of Christian history the price of conscience was death. In the 1940's that was the price Bonhoeffer paid. Martin Luther King paid it in 1968. Yet between Simon Peter and Dietrich Bonhoeffer and King, men like Tertullian and Augustine, Aquinas and Luther, Calvin and Cromwell managed to live responsibly with the conflicting claims of church and state.

The hard truth is that there are no fixed, absolute answers on the crucial issue before us, however much we yearn for them. Socrates, Plato, Aristotle, Locke, and Jefferson failed to reconcile personal liberty with the state's authority. Hobbes and Lenin, ignoring personal liberty, simply argued the state's case. "To face the problem of Man vs. the State is to recognize the uniform failure of political philosophy to solve it—or even to confront it." [14]

Jesus provides the most realistic approach: a man's conscience and the communal demands of his culture—his personal liberty and the state's authority—exist in tension; each person must decide allegiances and loyalties and establish priorities for himself in the dynamic context of his loyalty to God, his concern for humanity, and the ambiguities of history. More than that would be tyranny of the human spirit. Less than that would be irresponsibility to God, self, and society.

We shall examine several practical implications of this conclusion with reference to ecology in the next chapter.

[14] Mayer, *On Liberty*, p. 17.

*Democracy is much broader than a special political form, a method of conducting government, of making laws and carrying on governmental administration by means of popular suffrage and elected officers. It is that, of course. But it is something broader and deeper than that. The political and governmental phase of democracy is a means, the best means so far found, for realizing ends that lie in the wide domain of human relationships and the development of human personality. It is, as we often say, though perhaps without appreciating all that is involved in the saying, a way of life, social and individual. The keynote of democracy as a way of life may be expressed, it seems to me, as the necessity for the participation of every mature human being in formation of the values that regulate the living of men together: which is necessary from the standpoint of both the general social welfare and the full development of human beings as individuals.*

—John Dewey

# V

# CAN MAN CONTROL HIS CONTRIBUTION TO THE ENVIRONMENT?

A half century ago, a popular ditty asked, "How're you gonna keep 'em down on the farm after they've seen Paree?" And they didn't!

Today that tune could carry a basket of questions: How can one have clean air with 101,000,000 internal combustion engines and thousands of smoke-spewing factories? How can one expect quiet in a world of jets, high performance autos, and riveters? How can one have scenic roadways and clean streets when "the pause that refreshes" and "the champagne of beers" come in cans, when cigarettes and snacks are packaged in disposable containers, and when a single issue of the Sunday paper is thick enough to choke a rhinoceros? How can one preserve forests when "Smokey the Bear" is able to patrol only one section of one forest at any one time? How can one have fresh rivers when sprawling industries use them as cheap dumping grounds?

The answers to these questions have been increasingly negative. In fact, the questions were ignored until recently. Coleridge's familiar line, amended and expanded, describes the current environmental crisis: "Water, water everywhere, and not a pure drop to drink; nor pure air to breathe; nor natural scenery to enjoy; nor proper food to eat; nor adequate space to live in."

The initial draft of this chapter was sketched out on "Earth Day," April 22. That evening the Huntley-Brinkley Report devoted the major portion of its time to the public demonstrations in New York City, Cleveland, Chicago, Los Angeles, and Miami. It closed with exciting scenes from the protected natural beauty of the Cotswald in England. Several days earlier, *Look's* lead article had committed some dramatic observations to cold print.

> Earth Day, April 22, marks a time of warning. We are fouling our streams, lakes, marshes. The sea is next. We are burying ourselves under 7 million scrapped cars, 30 million tons of waste paper, 48 billion discarded cans and 28 billion bottles and jars a year. A million tons more of garbage pile up each day. The air we breathe circles the earth 40 times a year, and America contributed 140 million

tons of pollutants: 90 million from cars—we burn more gasoline than the rest of the world combined—15 million from electric power generation, one-third of the world's total. Lead in San Diego's air gets deposited in layers on the Pacific. L.A. smog may cause mass deaths by 1975. Noise, straining our lives, doubles in volume every ten years. There are 5,500 Americans born each day; 100 million more by 2000. We already consume and waste more than any other people. We flatten hills, fill our bays, blitz our wilderness. The quality drains from our lives; I am one-twenty-millionth of a swelling megalopolis. On Earth Day, Americans young and old are coming together for a national teach-in to talk about our wrecked earth. Environment Action, a group of fired-up college kids, is coordinating the teach-in. But after Earth Day, the talk and warning end, because THE FIGHT TO SAVE AMERICA STARTS NOW.[1]

President Nixon, silent on the environmental crisis during his campaign, issued a firm call on February 12, 1970, for "total mobilization" against pollution. Two months later, he looked benignly on the Earth Day demonstrators whose student leader had spurned the President's invitation to the White House. *The Environmental Handbook,* official source-book for the first national teach-in on ecology, provided a frightening collection of factual articles by America's first-rank scientists, historians, sociologists, economists, writers, and concerned students.[2] The church also showed signs of awareness.[3] Earth Day brought together parents, teachers, politicians, clergy, and young people in peaceful gatherings across the nation. One young man, assessing Establishment support, observed puckishly: "We must be doing something wrong!"

[1] *Look,* April 16, 1970.

[2] *The Environmental Handbook,* ed., Garrett DeBell (New York: Ballantine Books, 1970).

[3] See Frederick Elder's *Crisis in Eden* (Nashville: Abingdon Press, 1970), and *The Lutheran Forum,* April, 1970.

Actually, the young people and a cadre of their teachers (college and high school) did a number of things right. We shall examine several of their thrusts at a later point in this presentation.

The national teach-in on the Crisis of the Environment—which turned out to be meaningful in most communities—was the brain child of Senator Gaylord Nelson. The Senator also offered to the Senate this agenda on ecology for the 1970's.

Adoption of a constitutional amendment "which will recognize and protect the inalienable rights of every person to a decent environment."

Acting immediately by moving against the heaviest polluters by phasing out the internal combustion automobile engine by January 1, 1978; eliminating persistent, toxic pesticides by 1972; adopting antipollution standards for detergents; reducing jet aircraft pollution; and eliminating nonreturnable bottles, jars and cans by the development of reusable or degradable containers.

Establish and protect the right of every citizen to plan his family and make funds available for research into population problems and provide family planning service.

Creation of a citizen environmental advocate agency to involve citizens in environmental decision making and creation of an environmental overview committee in Congress.

Establishing an environmental education program that will make the environment and man's relationship to it the major subject of every level of public education.

Setting up a national policy on land use to stop chaotic and unplanned urban sprawl.

Establishing a national minerals and resources policy.

Setting a national air and water quality policy by closing the environmental money gap by giving full funding to present pollution control programs.

Launching a broad-scale effort to halt sea pollution by forbidding municipalities and industries to dump waste into the ocean, and declaring a moratorium on new leases or permits for all production and other activities on the undersea outer continental shelf until criteria are established for its protection.[4]

If this agenda, or any substantial part of it, is to become operational in American society, the ingrained attitudes of a comfort-rooted, production-minded, GNP-oriented citizenry must be changed radically and quickly. If this nation expects to resolve the escalating environmental crisis, "every person must develop a new ethical sense of his relationship to and his dependence upon the natural world. . . . We're all in the battle. In the immortal words of Pogo, quoted about every other day on this newly popular subject: 'We have met the enemy and they is us.' "[5] When we Americans discover not only the enormity of the task but also that the enemy "is us" instead of "them," many may lose their newfound interest in "the care of the earth."

This is a legitimate fear. It is a matter of record that Americans proved themselves to be more adept with words than deeds during the 50's and 60's. A substantial bloc of the citizenry had declared war against (1) racial inequality, (2) urban ghettoes, (3) poverty, (4) nuclear warfare, (5) ineffective and undemocratic public schools, (6) traffic congestion; but to date, the results have been slim. One reason is that too many expected too much, too soon. The hard reality is that man is slothful in fostering any idea or program which he does not recognize immediately as being beneficial to him. Man's vision and compassion are corrupt. He

[4] *Commission on Undergraduate Education in the Biological Sciences*, VI (March 1970), 3 (referred to hereafter as CUEBS).

[5] Victor Cohn, "But Who Will Pay the Piper and Will It Be in Time?" *Smithsonian* I 16-17. Mr. Cohn is science editor of the *Washington Post* and writes a regular column for the *Technology Review*, MIT.

does not recognize readily that short-term gains for himself, accomplished at the expense of others, throw his natural and social environment out of balance. Man has been exploiting nature since he picked the apple in the Garden of Eden. That act of human rebellion—presented in the form of myth in the Bible—provides a sobering perspective on man's disposition to despoil his environment and the difficulties which will overwhelm him if he relies primarily on an emotional approach to solve the current "crisis in Eden." Americans have a thin sense of evil, assume readily that they are rational, and rarely examine their motives. Those are the elemental reasons why "the typical pattern of the New American Crusade is words followed by ill-funded and inadequate programs followed by disillusionment followed by apathy." [6]

America has come to her moment of ecological truth with frightening tardiness. The first recorded air pollution disaster occurred almost a quarter of a century ago in a little mill town in western Pennsylvania, Donora. Only baseball buffs know the name of the town: Stan (the Man) Musial grew up there. An Associated Press writer did a piece on that "ancient" disaster for Earth Day. Excerpts from it are germane to the current national interest in ecology.

> At first, it was just another autumn fog that rolled in off the Monongahela River. . . . There was no indication of the choking menace that would blot out the sun for five days and bring this western Pennsylvania mill town to its knees.
>
> For most of the 12,000 residents on that Wednesday, Oct. 27, 1948, thoughts were elsewhere. . . .
>
> Elections were a week away. The baseball season had been over for three weeks and the town's native son, Stan Musial

[6] *Ibid.*, p. 15.

of the St. Louis Cardinals, had had another fantastic season, leading the league in batting with a .376 average.

The U.S. Weather Bureau reported dispassionately that a high-pressure system had created a temperature inversion—cold, dense air was trapped in the valley beneath a layer of warm air.

It also trapped the tons of soot, fumes and smoke that poured out of the stacks of a steel mill and zinc works, from chimneys, auto exhausts, trains, and passing boats.

The scene was set for America's first recorded air pollution disaster.

The statistics: twenty dead; 5,910 persons, or 42.7 percent of those living in the area, were sickened, including 1,440 who were severely ill.

The health department identified some of the pollutants as sulfur, nitrogen oxides, chlorides, flourides, arsenic, antimony, lead, cadmium, zinc, iron, manganese and acid gases.

It said the pollutants came from the mills, 2,300 other buildings that burned coal or oil for heat, an average of 22 boats a day that passed on the river, 18 freight trains, and six passenger trains, 10 switch engines and an estimated 3,000 automobiles that burned an estimated 26,000 pounds of fuel a day. . . .[7]

But the Donora mill workers in 1948 had become accustomed to polluted air. Like their fathers, they endured it because "smoke-filled skies" in the valley "meant full lunch pails." The same attitude prevails today in other chemically polluted industrial cities. Driving south of Chicago to meet a commitment for the Chicago Sunday Evening Club eleven days before Earth Day, I was depressed by the smog which darkened

[7] Greensburg (Pennsylvania) *Tribune-Review*, April 16, 1970.

a sunny spring sky. But a laborer who houses his family in the midst of that pollution (Gary, Indiana) was reconciled to it. He declared flatly: "Hell, it means $5.50 an hour to me." I could afford to be depressed; my family is not immediately dependent on the mills of Gary. The problem of eliminating pollution is complex because the personal-social situation is ambiguous. From the beginning (the formation of crude instruments and the cultivation of crops) to the present (the SST plane and moon landings), technology has benefitted some at the expense of others.

Flying into Philadelphia on a bright spring day in 1970, from twenty miles out, I saw dimly the city of Brotherly Love through a thick smog. In December, 1969, the Municipal Court had fined Philadelphia Electric Co., General Smelting Co., and Celotex Corp., alleged air pollution violators, a total of twelve dollars for their offense against society. *The Philadelphia Inquirer* noted that these particular firms had been named previously "among the fifteen major sources of air pollution identified by the city" in 1969.[8] Realistic laws are useless without the public's will to enforce them. Shortly after Earth Day a representative group of students and professors from academic communities of Philadelphia announced that they would provide concerned citizens of metropolitan Philadelphia with the names of polluting industries and agencies in their immediate neighborhoods. That will get results *if* the citizens want to be informed, decide to act in concert, and pay the cost. The environmental situation is ambiguous. That does not mean that it is hopeless. Aroused scientist-citizen coalitions in other places have proven to be effective.

During 1967, the Georgia Conservancy, Incorporated,

[8] Cited by Cohn, "But Who Will Pay the Piper?" p. 18.

was established to preserve areas of scenic beauty, to develop regional land-use planning, and to educate the citizenry in conservation needs and practice. The Conservancy, with strong citizen support, managed to reverse "the decision by political forces in league with a manufacturing plant (Kerr–McGee) to locate a phosphate mining operation in the estuaries on the east coast of Georgia and caused the state to declare two areas . . . as natural areas to be preserved for scientific, educational, and aesthetic purposes."[9]

*Pollution Probe* is a citizens' group of 1,300 students, professors, and concerned citizens which was organized at the University of Toronto. Its headquarters are in the zoology department there. *Probe,* concentrating on natural lakes, zeros in on the detergent industry. The group recommends that citizens demand government bans on phosphate detergents by 1972, and cut down immediately in their use of high phosphate detergents. They have published phosphate analyses of popular detergents.[10] They expect to achieve significant results. An aroused citizenry, intelligently organized, can get results in a representative form of government. Proof of that is that almost one fourth of the bills before the California Assembly in early 1970 dealt with pollution control.[11]

But will citizens in various nations go for the long haul? When Americans realize that effective action to recover and protect their natural environment will reduce their creature comforts, cost hundreds of billions of tax dollars, restrict "free enterprise," require planned towns, and necessitate an "allowance" on how many

[9] CUEBS, VI (March, 1970), 8.

[10] Yvonne Horton, "Facts and Figures to Aid in the Prevention of Water Pollution," *The Christian Science Monitor,* April 28, 1970.

[11] Cohn, "But Who Will Pay the Piper?" p. 17.

children future parents may have, will the current enthusiasm for the ecological crusade wane?[12] After all, the Donora disaster and the hundreds of subsequent smog deaths in Los Angeles, New York, and London during the 50's and 60's have awakened only sporadic concern in America or England. Existing pollution laws are enforced lightly or not at all. Forty-seven years ago (1924), 1,500 people in Greater New York suffered from various forms of gastroenteritis and 150 persons died due to polluted oysters. The great "oyster scare" caused the federal government to investigate the situation. A half century later "this Federal interest has not yet been translated into prevention. People are still suffering and dying from polluted sea food. . . . Too often, federal protection has seemed to be more readily available to the polluters than to the public."[13]

Demographers predict the need for zero population growth by A.D. 2000, yet many couples continue to have too many babies. It is not likely that the masses will endorse twenty-one-year-old Stephanie Mills' solution to the population explosion which she announced in her valedictory address at Mills College in 1969: she would not bring *any* children into "this muddled world." The population pressures which threaten the quality of life force into the arena of public debate the current contention that voluntary contraceptive services (including abortion and sterilization) must be made available to all people. The moral and practical implica-

[12] Responsible economists estimate that it would cost 120 billion a year simply to keep environmental deterioration gradual in *our* industrial society.

[13] "Can Doctors Cope With Man's New Environment?" A *Medical World News Reprint* (New York: McGraw-Hill, 1970), pp. 24-25.

tions of that thrust are widely controversial. Inertia and ignorance, as well as selfishness, prevent people from deciding for the quality of life against the quantity of life. Human beings, shortsighted, are loathe to change their ways of living voluntarily. It is a matter of historical record, for example, that London had a smog problem from burning soft coal in its crowded wooden houses as far back as 1285! [14] But soft coal provided a steadier heat than logs; it was more convenient and more comfortable. It is human nature to resist change when it inconveniences one, challenges his creature comforts, threatens his insecure person, or lays siege to his pocketbook.

We seem unable to manage change; we appear only to react to change. In a highly technological society with brilliant environmental scientists such as Eugene Odum, Barry Commoner, and Paul Ehrlich, we manage to turn deaf ears to their warnings. Seven years ago Rachel Carson warned us about the dangers of pesticides, yet it was not until the levels of DDT affected the economy of the salmon industry in Michigan or the crab industry of California that bills were introduced to ban the sale, use, or possession of persistent pesticides.[15]

The will to change and to persevere in a course of new action is the elemental problem in ecology today. It has been for decades. But what *has* been, if persisted in, could obliterate the human species or make humane life impossible by the end of this century. The enormity of the task comes into focus when we appraise the need for radical changes in private and public attitudes,

[14] Lynn White, Jr., "The Historical Roots of Our Ecological Crisis," *The Environmental Handbook*, p. 14.

[15] John D. Withers, CUEBS staff biologist, "Where Is the Problem?", CUEBS VI (March 1970).

educational aims, and governmental concern and action.

## *PRIVATE AND PUBLIC ATTITUDES*

Dr. John D. Withers, staff biologist, Commission on Undergraduate Education in the Biological Sciences, declares bluntly:

> The historical roots of our ecological crisis are constituted in Judeo-Christian tradition, since western man has been imbued with a perception of nature in which air, land, and water are exploitable because they are assumed to have been created to serve his purpose. This tradition tells us that man is for the glory of God, but I would submit that the same is true for all creations of The Creator.[16]

That sweeping judgment is larded with substantial truth. A scholarly examination of this ingrained exploitative attitude in Western society is provided by Dr. Lynn White, Jr., professor of history at the University of California. His carefully researched presentation is sobering for Catholics, Protestants, Jews, humanists, and scientists.[17] Briefly this is his argument.

The current rape of the environment is a consequence not only of the industrial-technological revolution and the natural disposition of man to serve his own immediate interests, but also of the Judeo-Christian teaching that God, having created man, gave him dominion over all natural life (except human life) and admonished him to subdue the earth. This anthropocentric religion, in contrast to ancient paganism and current world religions, produced a dualism in man and nature which allowed him to exploit nature for his own pur-

[16] *Ibid.*
[17] White, *The Environmental Handbook*, pp. 12-26.

poses. Dr. White argues cogently that this ingrained attitudinal approach to the natural environment must be recognized and altered if an effective ecology is to be developed. Unquestionably, this strand in the Judeo-Christian view of man and the world has prevailed in Western society. But there is a dissenting view in Judeo-Christian culture.

Richard A. Baer, Jr., associate professor of religion at Earlham College, acknowledges the validity of historian White's analysis. However, Baer goes on to point out that biblical religion at a deeper level has always stressed God's concern that man should live in harmony with all creation:

> Too long Christians have interpreted the Genesis command to exercise dominion over the earth as a mandate to conquer and exploit nature. So long as man possessed little technological ability to modify his environment on a large scale, such an exploitative and utilitarian attitude was only mildly destructive. But today all this has changed. The biological dominance of modern man coupled with his massive technological capabilities constitutes an unprecedented threat to the survival of life and beauty on this planet.
>
> The Church must change too. Not a few biblical passages speak against belittling the importance of man's physical being or the value of the natural world. Christ not only came in the flesh but also devoted much of his ministry to healing the physically ill. Paul boldly proclaimed the resurrection of the body (I Cor. 15) and affirmed the redemption of nature as well as of man (Rom. 8). Isaiah (11:6-9; 35:1-10) looked forward to the healing of nature in the day of the Lord, and the author of Revelation (21:1) anticipated a new heaven and a new earth. The Law provided a sabbath rest for the land (Lev. 25:1-7) and for beasts of burden (Deut. 5:12-15) as well as for man.[18]

[18] Richard A. Baer, "Christian Responsibility in Man's Relationship to Nature," *Lutheran Forum*, IV (April, 1970), 6.

More than a decade ago, the Lutheran theologian, Joseph Sittler of the Chicago Theological Seminary, was calling technological man to a larger concern in "the care of the earth." But it was Frederick Elder who focused the issue sharply for critical minds in the church. Expanding a thesis written at the Harvard Divinity School into a 1970 book, *Crisis in Eden*, the Rev. Mr. Elder identifies and discusses fully the anthropocentrism in one creation account in Genesis.[19] Next, he points out that decades ago biblical scholars identified two creation stories written from two sources, J and P. In the J source, man is indeed dominant, but that "account is only one half of the creation witness." [20]

The P source, on the other hand, puts God, not man, at the center. In that account, man is given dominion (Gen. 1:29), but he is not handed a blank check on the environmental bank. God views his whole creation as good and trusts man to exercise responsible stewardship over it. This theocentric view provides no ground for exploitation.[21] C. F. D. Moule, in his 1961 publication *Man and Nature in the New Testament*, defines the issue in two pithy sentences. "He (man) is meant to have dominion over it (world) and use it . . . but only for God's sake, only like Adam in paradise, cultivating it for the Lord. As soon as he . . . reaches out to take the fruit which is forbidden by the Lord, instantly the ecological balance is upset and nature begins to groan." [22]

The church through the ages neglected God in na-

[19] Elder, *Crisis in Eden*, p. 83.
[20] *Ibid.*, p. 85.
[21] *Ibid.*, pp. 83-104 convey Elder's sound argument.
[22] *Ibid.*, quoted p. 87.

ture. It still does. Its major theologians have concentrated their energies on "God in history" (the nature and meaning of revelation) and "God in personal experience" (conversion, ethical decisions, and existentialism). But the church's theologians have lagged badly in inquiring into "God in nature" (exploitation of natural resources by persons, agencies, and corporations; pollution control; cheapening and destruction of natural scenery; prayer in the light of the "new" physics; psychosomatic medicine, etc.). The mounting environmental crisis demands that we examine carefully the balance of nature before we blow everything up, exhaust the earth's resources, or pollute all life. It is man, violating God's order, who releases the four horsemen of the Apocalypse, plague, pestilence, famine, and death. Some scientists judge that one ten thousand megaton bomb could usher in another Ice Age. The greed for financial gain and neurotic concern for national security are luring modern man into building his own Tower of Babel. Nonetheless, the times are particularly hospitable for searching inquiries and cooperative ventures sponsored by Christians and secularists. The new science and the new theology provide a fresh intellectual climate for serious dialogue; the failure of atheistic rationalism, benign humanism, and ecclesiastical theology to improve the lot of all people points up the need for dialogue; a growing openness between churchmen and agnostic intellectuals offers hope for a fruitful encounter. The church should move out "on the double." Biblical theology and scientific ecology are allies.

It is imperative then that the church enlarge its conception and practice of stewardship to include "the care of the earth." The need for a wider and more realistic sense of private and public trusteeship is urgent. Elder joins Galbraith, Gardner, McGovern, Muskie, and others in calling for it. Specifically, he suggests a modern-day asceticism which orients to these demands: "(1) restraint, (2) an emphasis upon quality existence, and (3) reverence for life." [23] Elder urges the church to take the lead in ecological reform. He argues that since a change in man's attitude "involves nothing less than a conversion . . . , the churches are best equipped to carry out this sort of thing. . . ." [24]

The church must indeed accept responsibility for persuading people to become concerned environmentalists, but it cannot do the task alone. Education and government must also be motivated to act or ecology will end as a fad. Enlightenment must be provided in and through the public schools and skills must be developed in the colleges and universities. A large-scale program initiated by our representative government—local, state, and federal—is equally essential to an effective care of the earth. Technology, corporate capitalism, and human selfishness, more than a careless interpretation of the Judeo-Christian scriptures and tradition, have produced today's ecological crisis.

This appraisal, however, does not excuse the church from facing the environmental problem as a theological problem. Serious reflection on and addressment to the environment is one Christian concern among others.

But the church, like other institutions of society, must guard against taking up the "crisis in Eden" as an escape from the unresolved and socially divisive issues of race, poverty, and peace. After all, the care of the earth and the struggle for the dignity of man are complementary aspects of biblical religion. An enlightened self-interest is not a matter for apology among

[23] *Ibid.*, p. 145 ff.
[24] *Ibid.*, pp. 161-62.

ardent liberals; it is a biblical mandate. God is more pragmatic, given ultimates, than man. He is universally concerned; man is parochially concerned. The modern American, instead of consuming without thought, must learn to purchase discriminately, to forego some of his creature comforts, to conserve, and to recycle. But will affluent teenagers and their fathers give up their 350-400 h.p. autos? Will mothers use canvas bags for shopping? Will Americans recognize and alter their economy of glut?

## *EDUCATION*

Those who appreciate imaginative teaching will be gratified to learn that there is a young college professor who introduces his course in population control by requiring his students to fast for five days on water alone. An experience like that can engender a personal identification with starving people everywhere, at least for a few days.

But ecological reform requires more than simulated empathy.

Unless high school and college people move beyond the emotionalism which goes in for gimmicks, buttons, posters, and rallies and tackle the unglamorous task of studying ecological relationships in such depth that some students will become professional specialists, while others will become knowledgeable enough as amateurs to work effectively on ecology in their communities for the next fifty years, today's student generation and their professors will make little contribution to ecological reform. Without trained talents in-depth, society hasn't a ghost of a chance of overmatching the environmental crisis in the next several decades. Conversion without enlightenment and effective skills will not resolve the environmental crisis.

*Can Man Hope to Be Human?*

Dr. Donald S. Dean identifies four essential challenges which educators, students, and society must meet.

First, if the problems of man's survival in a decent kind of world are to be solved, the solution must be accomplished by people with the intellectual skills to analyze the problems and to do what is necessary to solve them. We have a responsibility to cultivate these skills in our students.

We must develop in students a zest for attacking problems and help them gain the intellectual tools to accomplish the attack. Education must not continue to require the passive acceptance of a huge body of organized facts, but by the same token, education must not be identified with the passive acceptance of soul-stirring diatribes. We must develop in our students a passion for truth and a disdain for sloppy argument even when put forth in the name of a worthy cause. . . .

Second, many of the problems of man do not presently have an obvious solution. It will take well-educated people in a number of fields to make the discoveries which will make it possible for man to continue on this earth. The person who will find some substitute for the internal combustion engine or some way for man to live with it must know some mathematics. It will not suffice for him to carry a placard denouncing air pollution. It will take a good knowledge of genetics—some not even known today—to develop some of the food plants and animals needed. . . .

Unless someone is equipped to understand the human being better than he is understood today, our cities will continue to erupt in violence. Worse yet is the probability that people living in this increasingly crowded world will become resigned to the regimentation and restriction of their freedom of choice that such crowding inevitably brings, unaware that there could be a better world. If this is not to happen, someone had better do his homework in sociology, in psychology, in city planning, in urban ecology, and in education. . . . There will be no substitute for knowledge in the solution of our problems of survival. . . .

Third, there is a certain amount of information about our world that should be part of the equipment of all citizens if they are to fulfill their role as custodians of our environment. If there were no crisis in the environment, it would still be necessary for a well-informed citizen to understand the finiteness of this earth and the way materials are cycled back for use again and again. They need to understand the intricate interrelationship of all living things in the environment which sustains them. There must be developed in all of our students an appreciation of life—especially human life—based squarely on a knowledge of life and living things.

Finally, we must recognize the scope of the problem and the wholeness of the problem. The quality of the human environment is not just a biological problem; it involves the whole spectrum of human concerns. . . .

If we neglect to give real substance to our studies, ecology, population, and environment will go the same way as familiar cant words that have flashed across the scene.[25]

Is the present system of education flexible enough to meet these challenges? Dr. Dean is calling for an end to fragmented learning. He is calling for "a new oneness" in education. This would require a radical recasting of curricula, the development of team and group teaching, and a new awareness of our common humanity and environment. Public and private education cannot manage this without basic changes in its philosophy, economic help from foundations, and billions of tax dollars from the government.

## *GOVERNMENT*

The unvarnished truth is that government (local, state, federal) must enforce vigorously the present laws

[25] Donald S. Dean, staff biologist, CUEBS, VI (March, 1970), 21.

on ecology, frame tougher laws and enforce them equitably, and place billions of dollars at the disposal of ecological specialists in and outside industry. Otherwise, the environmental crisis will worsen. But many concerned people—reviewing critically the government's past unwillingness and inability to resolve the crises of race, poverty, war, urban ghettoes, and transportation in this nation—have lost confidence in the political system in America. Remembering the demonstrations, riots, violence, and death which have marked the grass-roots quest for racial justice and an end to the war in Indo-China, many youth and their parents have decided that bureaucratic government offers no hope.

Yet there is another side to this. The government *is* wrestling with civil rights, poverty, extrication from Indo China, etc. It has begun to tackle environmental control. Its massive failures and its small successes on all these fronts testify to a partial willingness to cope with social, economic, and ecological changes. The failures are complexly rooted: the enormity and blinding tempo of social change; but more, the attitudes, working knowledge, and imagination of the legislators *and* the electorate. When Woodrow Wilson was president of Princeton University, a critical alumni gathering asked, "Why doesn't Princeton do more for our sons?" Wilson answered with acerbity, "Because they are your sons."

Municipal, state, and federal legislators are the *people's* representatives. They reflect majority and/or vocal attitudes among their constituencies. Labor and management, adults and youth (except for a minority among both), white and black, educated and uneducated want a piece of the economic action in our affluent society. Unchecked economic growth (more jobs and a higher material standard of living) has been the goal not only of industrial management and local Chambers of Commerce but equally of the American people. The time has come for each to ask: How much do I need and how comfortable must I be and at whose expense am I advanced? These are not rhetorical questions. They explain one strand in the government's Fabian approach to explosive social issues. Senator Edmund Muskie, a vigorous ecologist, criticized President Nixon's niggardly recommendation for funds to improve the environment; but the Senator's own recommendation was, in view of the job to be done, equally inadequate. Both politicians recognize that the taxpayer's ire is white hot. A sound course would be to reorder our national priorities. But most Americans are not inclined to reconsider the priorities which determine the current use of federal tax dollars.

The call for a new asceticism toward material things, for self-discipline, for empathy, for compassion, for reverence toward life is a century late in America. There is pressing need among the citizenry to grasp the full meaning of that old Chinese proverb: "If your shoe has a hole in it, my foot is cold." Until we Americans accept and orient concretely to the basic truth that we must act toward others as we want them to act toward us, we shall treat humans as objects and objects as gods; and we shall support governmental policies which reflect that self-interest. Americans need desperately to develop a humane philosophy. Specifically, American churchmen need to outgrow their ego-centered religion and commit themselves to God-centered religion. American citizens need motivation in depth and enlightenment in breadth. American society is foundering for want of ethical religion, insight-producing education, and creative political action.

Ideologically, the American government is fashioned

to serve all its citizens. In its present bureaucratic form it goes about this task ineptly and sluggishly. It responds tardily and inadequately to the pressures generated by cascading social-economic-political changes at home and abroad. It reacts to violent changes more than it acts to produce salutary change. Our basic political philosophy is sound, but our political forms are not well adapted to the demands of an industrial-technological society in a revolutionary world. We possess a Constitution which can be interpreted flexibly and relevantly. We can also amend it responsibly. We can fashion a government which helps people to realize their humanity. Able minds, young and adult, from all fields of endeavor must give a measure of their energies (full-time in some cases) if the present bureaucratic government is to be transformed into a government of, by, and for the people. Political action provides a viable means for creating social and environmental situations which are hospitable to man. That is the profound political truth which John Kennedy enunciated when he declared, "Ask not what your country can do for you; ask what you can do for your country." In a totalitarian state, Mr. Kennedy's declaration would have been authoritarian—the state above man. In a politically representative society it was (and is) an invitation to the citizens to fashion a government which intends to, can, and does encourage and enable people to become human—the State for man. Most Americans need a fresh sense of the crucial place of politics in contemporary life as well as attitudinal conversion and continuing enlightenment on the realities of their social and natural environment.[26]

[26] See Wallace E. Fisher, *The Affable Enemy* (Nashville: Abingdon Press, 1970), pp. 73-141, for an account of a fictional churchman's discovery of and participation in politics as a viable means to reorder society.

*Can Man Control His Contribution to the Environment?*

In the context of this and the preceding chapter it is easy to be concrete about the complexities of ecological politics. On Tuesday, May 5, 1970, the Chevron Oil Co. was indicted on 900 counts arising from a massive off-shore oil spill. According to an AP release it is the first action of its kind on record.[27] Conviction on all counts could result in a total fine of 1.8 million dollars. Secretary of the Interior, Walter J. Hickel, who had asked for the grand jury probe, promised to be "fair but tough." K. H. Shaffer, President of Chevron, announced, "We are confident that when the case is tried, we will be completely vindicated." [28] Vested interests, on their own initiative, do not divest themselves of profit and power. That is the theme of Reinhold Niebuhr's *Moral Man and Immoral Society.* The motivation for change must come from outside. And *that* is part of the problem in affluent America.

Will the American consumer decide to pay more for gasoline (at least immediately) or stand by uncaring until oil spews into the Gulf of Mexico for another twenty-one days? Who will the citizenry support, not only in this case but in future cases, a courageous government official or a competent representative of corporate free enterprise?

On June 10, 1970, *The Christian Century* editorialized on the failure of concerned persons to get General Motors shareholders to endorse a "Shareholders' Committee for Corporate Responsibility" which would monitor GM's efforts to produce safer and nonpolluting automobiles. "Campaign GM" lost by a landslide. The efforts of Ralph Nader, consumer advocates, environmentalists and a few churchmen to make the world's largest corporation more responsive to the claims of

[27] *New Era* (Lancaster, Pennsylvania), May 6, 1970, p. 31.
[28] *Ibid.*

public safety, health and welfare were swamped by the votes in the hands of General Motors' managers." [29] Although Boston University supported Campaign GM, Harvard, MIT, Princeton, and Columbia declined to do so. Denominational and interdenominational church bodies gave their votes to Campaign GM, but the weight of their support was negligible.

Since 1950, the total number of stockholders in the United States has increased from 6 million to 26 million. These decent people obviously prefer "to share in the profits" rather than "to share in the responsible use of power." [30] Only the federal government is powerful enough to cope with the corporate giants. And the exercise of that capability depends substantially on the electorate.

If the environmental crisis is addressed seriously, American consumers will have to pay more for less and American citizens will have to pay more taxes or work diligently to convince their representatives that they really want to reorder governmental priorities radically. On the other hand, if this crisis is ignored or even neglected, the next generation will inherit an exhausted, polluted, scarred earth. And that spells death. Planets, like men, wear out and die. So far as science can determine, the earth is the only planet in this universe capable of sustaining life. And all life is a one-shot enterprise. It is nonrepeatable. God intends and human concern requires that man care for all life responsibly. "Now is the time for all good men to come to the aid of their planet." [31] "Some wonder whether it will be the sounds of nuclear explosion or the 'silent

[29] *The Christian Century,* June 10, 1970, p. 715.
[30] *Ibid.*
[31] *Time,* June 1, 1970, p. 5.

spring' that will end it all, the bang or the whimper." [32]

The searing challenge of ecology, like other contemporary social challenges, is not a "safe" issue. It cannot be met without creating tension, stirring controversy, and engendering conflict. Unless man accepts and learns to work creatively with conflict in a world society in process of change, man's future estate will be worse than his present estate.

Since the church has a theology of conflict and reconciliation, it is the one institution which should lead in helping people to face, engage in, and handle conflict creatively. In fact, it has a mandate from God to do that. The theme of the next chapter is reconciliation through conflict.

[32] Gabriel Fackre, address at the Lancaster Theological Seminary, April 22, 1970.

*Theologically, the fact of conflict is an extremely simple inference from the doctrine of original sin. This much-maligned doctrine may be taken at the very least to mean that man is almost unavoidably self-centered. Self-interest appears to be the most dominant human motivation, and when the interests of different individuals clash, conflict ensues. Reinhold Niebuhr has given one of the most cogent descriptions of man's conflict-producing nature. In* Moral Man and Immoral Society, *he rebutted the bland optimism of the Social Gospel by demonstrating that humans, particularly in their group life, are inevitably caught up in the clash of self-interest. Paul Tillich, in* Love, Power, and Justice, *has echoed this finding and attempted to reveal its metaphysical rootage. In his opinion, love must be complemented by power that seeks to destroy that which is against love. Even the exponents of "reconciliation" recognize that there must be conflict before reconciliation can be had.*

—Robert Lee

# VI

# CAN CONFLICT EVER BE CHRISTIAN?

Tension, controversy, and conflict are elemental strands in the Christian life. That is incontrovertibly true because it is life and because commitment to Christ involves a cross. Conflict develops when man pits his will against God's will. Controversy emerges when people constrained to seek humane goals in actual situations collide with people bent on serving personal or parochial interests. Tensions arise when committed people who are agreed on goals collide with one another over methodology and tempo.[1]

Conflict is a dominant theme in scripture from the Garden of Eden to the Garden of Gethsemane, from the fleshpots of Egypt to the Cross outside Jerusalem. The fact that Christ demonstrated humanity's possibilities and provided the means to realize those possibilities actually magnifies tension and conflict initially for those who take him seriously. Jesus made that clear: "Think not that I came to bring peace, but a sword." Truth and falsehood collide. Human egos pursuing their own interests collide. Social classes, cultural groups, sovereign states, and races bent on achieving their own interests collide. That is life. Commitment to Christ often intensifies these tensions; frequently, it widens them into controversy and conflict. That is the Cross.

On one occasion Jesus rebuked Peter: "Out of my way, Satan! You stand right in my path, Peter, when you look at things from man's point of view and not from God's." (Matt. 16:23, Phillips) The gospel, the church, and the world cannot coexist without tension and conflict. It is generally agreed that the gospel is in conflict with materialism. It is not widely understood, however, that it is also in conflict with the institutional church: Paul's face-to-face encounter with Peter over the universal character of the gospel; the harsh controversy between the Docetists and the adherents of the Apostolic Faith (which produced the doctrine of the Incarnation); and presently, the attacks on Rome from within and the deepening cleavage between clergy and

[1] See Wallace E. Fisher, *Preface to Parish Renewal* (Nashville: Abingdon Press, 1966), chapter 5, for a critical examination of the church and conflict from the view of a parish pastor.

laity in Protestant churches. The gospel produces conflict in the church as well as in the world. The current peace-of-mind cult dominant in some quarters of the church is cultural, not biblical.

The Cross demonstrates dramatically that the inescapable conflict between light and darkness, truth and error, justice and injustice can be violent. It reveals what men will do to one another and to God to achieve their wrong-headed understanding of "good" purposes. Men have been doing harsh deeds in the name of truth for centuries. Socrates was poisoned by the "men of Athens." Caesar was knifed by a fellow senator. The crusades were rank with bigotry and greed. The religious wars in sixteenth- and seventeenth-century Europe were a long nightmare of intolerance and destruction. Here in the land of the free, Lincoln was shot in Ford's Theatre; John Kennedy was gunned down on the streets of Dallas; Martin Luther King was murdered on the balcony of the Lorraine Motel in Memphis.

But Jesus was murdered, too. The abuse and humiliation heaped on him, and the denials and rejection he suffered before his execution point up dramatically how man can devise evil means to achieve his own purposes, religious and political. How did it happen that a man as politically innocuous and as socially relevant as Jesus could receive a ticker-tape parade on Sunday, be victimized by a kangaroo court on Thursday, and suffer a Ku Klux Klan lynching on Friday? If we gain some insight into that question, we shall begin to understand that reconciliation in the Christian sense comes only through conflict.

## I

The conflict between Jesus and the religious-political establishment which ended in violence and death was not a burst of spontaneous combustion. Like the mob actions in 1970, that conflict had been brewing for a long time. The violence was the culmination of what had begun to happen as soon as Jesus took up his public ministry. It is important to recognize that the seeds of conflict were there from the beginning.

Jesus' first public act was to read the scripture in the synagogue in Nazareth, his home town. His pious fellow townsmen were delighted with their comely, devout neighbor. But when Jesus announced that Isaiah's prophecy was fulfilled in his person they turned on him viciously. He was forcibly ejected from the synagogue. He had to flee town to escape physical injury. The first time Jesus challenged the religious establishment to adopt a larger view of God and man, its leaders planted their feet firmly in the status quo.

That is what the Hebrew prophets had predicted would happen. After all, it had happened to them. They were not Nostradamuses! They were intelligent, sensitive, reflective men who related existentially to God and to history. When Jeremiah was rejected by his people because he spoke for God, he perceived that God was rejected too. Isaiah (II), remembering his harsh experiences in speaking for God, perceived that the Messiah would be not a Lordly King but a Suffering Servant, despised, humiliated, rejected. Mary was warned before Jesus' birth that her joy would be shattered by massive sorrow: "A sword shall pierce thy soul also." Jesus told his disciples plainly that the day would come when people would persecute and kill them in the name of God. The dehumanized society in the Roman world could not tolerate the gospel that challenged and motivated men to be human. Conflict was inevitable.

But at the outset of Jesus' ministry, it was others, not

he, who fanned the smoldering embers into that raging conflagration. The moment Jesus began to attract crowds—and that occurred quickly in his ministry—the religious leaders (Pharisees) placed him under surveillance. They were envious and fearful of his influence. As his fame spread they assigned additional agents to "watch him." They spied on his private activities. If there had been a phone in the home of Simon Peter's mother-in-law, where Jesus spent an occasional free day, the Pharisees would have had it tapped. At every "whistle-stop" in Jesus' itinerant ministry, people crowded in to hear him. The Pharisees, panicked by his snow-balling appeal ("the common people heard him gladly"), aware that his evangelical teaching threatened their traditional teaching (". . . but I say unto you . . ."), infuriated by his concern for the "wrong" people (publicans, sinners, tax collectors, adulteresses, Samaritans, Romans), maintained a round-the-clock security check on Jesus. They infiltrated his audiences, heckled him with devious questions, misquoted him shamelessly. No candidate for public office ever received more unfair "press coverage" than Jesus!

These were some of the loaded questions they hurled at him: "Do you consider yourself greater than Moses?" "Do you judge yourself to be above the law given at Sinai?" "Should we give allegiance to Caesar (state) or to God?" Each question was an intellectual minefield because it could be answered only in context. But Jesus declined to answer "off the record." He asked no immunity. He fielded every question with grace, clarity, and candor. Asked which of the moral laws is the greatest, Jesus replied plainly that the law could be summed up in a single sentence: "Love God with all your heart, mind, soul, and strength, and your neighbor as you love yourself." Pressed to answer, "Who is my neighbor?" Jesus responded by pointing out that one's neighbor is anyone who at anytime in any place experiences any human need (Good Samaritan). The Pharisees—furious with frustration, neurotically defensive, determined to undermine Jesus' influence—increased the tempo of their underhanded attacks, but only at the end did Jesus force them to show their true colors. Promptly, they demanded that he be tried for treason against the state, a crime punishable by death.

But the events which culminated in that political-religious trial and crucifixion had deeper causes than the petty, envious maneuverings of the religious elite. The Pharisees were "decent" people who honestly believed that their cause was just. They kept the moral law meticulously—that was their religion. Having divorced their religion from the prophetic tradition, they did not view righteousness in terms of justice and love between and among people but in terms of manners and religious rites. Jesus, recovering the prophetic tradition and going beyond its demands, taught that if a man's heart is right with God that man is justified. Faith and good works, worship and witness, are inseparable. Collision between these two views of God and man was inevitable. They could not coexist peaceably. They were, and are, in basic conflict. The issue was, and is, larger than the human participants.

But until the end, Jesus endeavored patiently to persuade the Pharisees to accept the authority of his Father. That is not to imply that he was naïve. "He knew what was in man." He was alert to the gathering storm. He pointed out the signs of it to his disciples and told them what would happen. But the disciples, failing to grasp the implications of his realistic counsel and to prepare themselves, went to pieces under the multiple pressures of that turbulent last week.

The time and place for open conflict was chosen by Jesus, the annual feast of the Passover when Jerusalem was crowded with pilgrims. It was then and there that Jesus elected to confront the religious establishment openly. Ignoring the counsel of his disciples, especially Peter, he set out for Jerusalem. He knew that he was heading for the final showdown. Superficially, Jesus' appearance in Jerusalem may remind some middle-aged Americans of the sheriff's lonely confrontation with the "baddies" in the cinema classic *High Noon*. Not so! The differences are cosmic: Jesus was not bent on being a hero (he was obeying God); and no one stood by Jesus at the last minute except God.

In contrast with the Pharisees who lurked in the shadows, Jesus did not slip quietly into the Holy City. He entered with fanfare. The crowds hailed him. Hosannas rolled down the streets. Quite deliberately Jesus precipitated a peaceful demonstration among the rank and file who thronged Jerusalem for the feast days. The donkey ride was not a cheap theatrical trick. It was symbolic; the long-awaited Messiah had come. In that sense, Jesus precipitated the conflict with the religious establishment and the political establishment.

Specifically, Jesus went directly to the Temple, the center of Phariseeism. This time he did not dialogue. He confronted his self-willed adversaries with the unvarnished accusation that they had turned God's house into a den of thieves. That stripped away the Pharisees' casuistry, deceit, hypocrisy. They stood exposed. Jesus had to be silenced; he had to die. So, they rushed to Pilate and Herod insisting that the state be the assassin. Under the threat of a civil revolt in Judea, the political forces (Jewish and Roman) joined ranks with the religious forces; Herod and Pilate struck a bargain. Justice was ignored; compassion grew cold; truth was nailed to the wall.

Down the centuries other unholy alliances between politicos and ecclesiastics have been formed when the power of both was being challenged. Constantine used the church to the state's advantage and his own. The medieval church manipulated the feudal lords to advance its secular power. Henry VIII and Elizabeth I, like Constantine, used the church to advance their personal and national interests. In eighteenth-century France, the church, long an arm of the state, suffered bitterly in the 1789 revolution. Colonial America, except for Pennsylvania and Virginia, was headed for the same fate when Jefferson pressed successfully for the amendment which separated the institutions of church and state. Every selfish alliance between church and state has destroyed eventually the order and peace it promised. That is history's testimony.

Pilate, the man, could not stomach the religionists who demanded that the state do their dirty work. He considered Jesus to be innocent of the charges brought against him, and said so. But Pilate was not willing to risk his person or his office for Jesus. He concocted an ingenious plan for freeing the Galilean. Following the custom which called for the release of a criminal at the Passover Feast each year, the Roman governor chose the meanest criminal in the cell block: a highwayman, an insurrectionist, a murderer, and set him alongside Jesus. Pilate reasoned that the crowd would direct that Jesus be freed. But the Pharisees, now openly hostile, would have none of that. They stirred the crowd to choose Barabbas. Masters of in-fighting, they inquired of Pilate, "Will you, a Roman governor, free a man who claims to be above Caesar?" "Is Pilate Caesar's friend?" *That* overrode the governor's sense of justice. Ambitious for political advancement, eager to escape the despised province of Judea on the outer edge of the Empire, Pilate decided against Jesus. Ceremoniously, he washed his hands of the deed and advised the Pharisees that the guilt was theirs. But Pilate had decided. It was the Roman governor who, possessing the power of life and death, turned the scale against Christ, truth, and humanity.

We have forgotten the great neutral *world of man* in which the crucifixion took place. We do not set it in the world . . . of hard realities. We set it in a curious void in which there are only God's chosen people and Jesus. Jesus comes to the chosen people and the chosen people reject him, all in the frame of a Bible story. Pilate changes the whole picture. He represents the wider world which involves Jesus and the Jews *together:* the wider world whose political realities *force* a "people of God" to explode itself in an ugly force.[2]

Pilate's decision by default remains a "respectable" way to avoid making life's hard moral decisions: "My corporation—my nation—my commanding officer—my church is to blame. I did only what I was expected to do. But, *I* am innocent." Adolph Eichmann made that plea. Lt. Calley made that plea. Bishop DeFregger made that plea. Lyndon Johnson made that plea. Richard Nixon makes that plea. Everyone makes that plea in one form or another, at one time or another.

Of course, the wider world of political and social realities forces all of us to make decisions occasionally that we would not otherwise have made. Every socio-political situation is ambiguous and potentially tragic. Nonetheless, it is true that if Pilate had

[2] Dom Sebastian Moore, *No Exit* (Paramus, N.J.: Paulist/Newman Press, 1968), p. 38.

been willing to lose his governorship, he could have acted on his honest judgment that Jesus should be freed. Tension, controversy, and conflict surface wherever Christ moves in this world because human beings are free to decide for or against him. *That* makes the cost of discipleship high. But only as man decides for truth and justice and mercy does he become truly human. That reality suggests the wider context in which tension breeds and conflict grows—human freedom.

## *II*

The crucifixion could not have happened if the people, exercising their freedom, had decided to support Jesus. Deciding for their own way of life, the Pharisees set out to erase Jesus' way of life. Pilate decided to protect his professional interests. The masses who had cheered Jesus on Sunday decided against costly personal involvement on Thursday. The disciples also decided that discretion was the better part of valor. Each of these decisions was made in the context of human freedom. Kierkegaard understood the cosmic significance of man's freedom; he called it "dreadful freedom."

Jesus also decided. The institutional church has not gotten that truth before its people in concrete terms. The Man from Nazareth was not programmed for Calvary. Jesus, bone of our bone, sinew of our sinew, flesh of our flesh, decided voluntarily to do the will of his Father whatever it cost him. Deeply rebellious in Gethsemane, Jesus nonetheless drank "the cup." Like any other man, he had to decide, and to reaffirm that decision periodically, whether he would discern and do God's will: the Temple at twelve, the Wilderness at thirty, the confrontation with Peter at thirty-two, the garden of Gethsemane hours before his trial and crucifixion, Golgotha as death crowded out his life. Jesus was not a spirit who appeared to be human. He was fully human. Like any other man he wrestled with his "dreadful freedom."

But the full meaning of the Crucifixion is not grasped simply by probing at the "historical" Jesus until the evangelists' brilliant portraits of faith are reduced to dull negatives. The "Jesus of history" is significant because the Risen Christ is in the midst of life now. Jesus is not locked in Jewish history like John the Baptist or in Roman history like Pontius Pilate. Scripture testifies historically to the event; and the Resurrected Christ is that event recurring in every moment of recorded time. The biblical report of God's saving deed in Christ is a historical report, but it is more than a report. The Christ-event, rooted in history, is not limited to any single period in history. The message of Christ, as Luther observed, "is to me not simply an old song about an event that happened fifteen hundred years ago . . . ; it is a gift and bestowing that endures forever." Christ shared Paul's stonings, beatings, shipwreck, trial, crucifixion. Christ participated in Luther's ordeal in the monastery. Christ walked to the gallows with Bonhoeffer on the 9th of April, 1945. No mortal handles his "dreadful freedom" alone, unless he decides to do so.

Two decades ago an American Black, uniquely talented and growing in his commitment to God and man, made a firm decision to work nonviolently for the liberation of blacks and other neglected people in American society. Martin Luther King—harassed in Montgomery, spit on in Selma, knifed in New York, jailed in Birmingham, killed in cold blood in Memphis —never swerved from his initial decision to serve humanity. But he had to reaffirm that decision periodically in the face of mounting tensions and deepening conflicts. He was not "programmed" for Memphis. He did not precipitate conflict there; he revealed it, uncovered it, and Christ was at his side.

Each man is free in every moment of his recorded time to say yes or no to the Way, the Truth, and the Life. And those who respond affirmatively in their freedom and renew that affirmation daily do not walk alone. So Paul declares in spite of stonings and beatings, frustration and humiliation, alienation and rejection: "Christ is appealing by me." So the church sings across the ages, "Greater good because of evil. . . ." Reconciliation in the Christian sense comes only through internal conflict ("O wretched man that I am.") and external conflict ("We wrestle not against flesh and blood but against the principalities of darkness").

Obviously, many people, exercising their freedom, do not embrace this conclusion. Some, caught in the same escalating evil that engineered Jesus' Cross, interpret life deterministically. They insist that human events are outside rational and moral control; God is powerless. Doris Day's lilting song, "What will be, will be" makes sense to them. Stoically, they accept life as it comes. They expect little, they hope for less. Other sensitive people—remembering how Jesus prayed that the cup would pass from him only to meet the hard silence of God—conclude with Albert Camus, "There is no choice," or with Nietzsche, "God is dead." Still others, experiencing personal Golgothas or brooding over a Golgotha which ripped a loved one to shreds, decide bitterly: "It's dog eat dog"; "To the victor belong the spoils"; "The race is not to the swift but to the clever." For them, God is impersonal, uncaring, cold.

Meanwhile, the Christ-followers go on seeking reconciliation through conflict as Jesus did. "No cross, no crown" is the way the devout Quaker, William Penn, put it. The life of faith is crowded with hurt and humiliation. The Cross engenders frustration, anguish, and doubt. Ethel Kennedy, holding to God, knows desperate days. Coretta King, committed to Christ, does not arise each morning singing, "Hallelujah!" Dietrich Bonhoeffer did not set out to get himself hanged at Flossenburg in 1945. The Christ-followers do not covet heroism. They do not wear shirts of hair. They do not seek conflict. The Christ-followers accept conflict and endure it and die under it if necessary to share in Christ's reconciliation of humanity to God.

Jesus did not court death. He loved life. He was not a religious masochist getting his emotional kicks from offering his body for crucifixion. He was not a swashbuckling adventurer who courted danger for the thrill of it. He was not a Western marshal whose ego required him to be a hero. Jesus loved life. He loved his family and his friends. He enjoyed good company and good food. Bourbon-drinking, cigar-smoking Churchill would have appreciated his company. Lincoln would have revelled in his stories. Theodore Roosevelt, sharing his zest for life, would have shouted, "Bully for you."

But they may not have appreciated, as many do not today, Jesus' single-minded efforts to liberate the captives, his unswerving labors to share the good news with the poor, and his dedication to do his Father's will at all times. His intense commitment to God created tension, precipitated controversy, and spawned conflict in a world where men want their own way strongly enough to oppose God's will. That is why Jesus warned men to count the cost of discipleship before they set out to follow him. He still does.

The reality that permeates the whole of Jesus' ministry is this: human life and history make sense because God has not given up on his world, is at work in it with those who love him, has turned it over to them in Christ. Acceptance of that reality means tension and conflict in one's person and with other persons because man stubbornly wants to have life on his own terms, not God's. Christian reconciliation is meaningless apart from conflict. This is empirically demonstrated in the daily news reports and in man's day-to-day relationships with his fellows and his social institutions. From many, we shall cite one contemporary example.

Several years ago (1966) the Presbyterians in the San Francisco Bay Area considered the possibility of bringing in Saul Alinsky to organize the residents in the ghetto area. The proposers intended to spend $200,000 in the venture. Throughout the church in that area, tension mounted; conflict broke out; churchmen shouted at churchmen; the in-fighting among church leaders was bitter. The proposal was defeated.[3] Dr. Robert Lee, professor of social ethics at the Presbyterian Seminary in San Anselmo, states that the Presbyterian church in the Bay Area became "so polarized that it may be called schizophrenic." [4]

Dr. Lee and several collaborators have provided a critical study of this fracas titled *The Schizophrenic Church*. This book was commissioned by the Board of Christian Education, United Presbyterian Church, U.S.A. Lee and his associates contend that the church

[3] Robert Lee, and Russell Galloway, *The Schizophrenic Church. Conflict over Community Organization* (Philadelphia: Westminster Press 1969).

[4] *Ibid.*, p. 165.

was severely split and the division has not yet healed. In addition to reporting on the in-fighting among Presbyterian church leaders, the co-authors provide detailed reports on how the controversy engulfed five local churches (fictitious names are used).

"Dr. Comfort of Pleasant Ridge Chruch," an ad interim pastor, decided to avoid all discussion of the issue. The report reveals that the parishioners in this church, unable to communicate with church leaders with whom they disagreed, were wholly alienated from them. Denied the opportunity for dialogue and discussion, the members let the conflict solidify their antagonism to the Presbyterian leaders. Reconciliation did not occur.

The study presents other conclusions which can help all congregations and judicatories. (1) Tension is an evidence of Christianity and not a disease. (2) Conflict is an evidence of the relevance of the doctrine of original sin (man is self-centered). (3) The church, moving into the political and social arenas under divine constraint, engenders conflict on many fronts. (4) The church must develop tools and methods for "conflict management." (5) Congregations and judicatories need permanent forums where conflicts can be brought into the open with adversaries confronting each other. (6) Conflict not only clears the air but often heals and binds the antagonists together.[5]

But the United Presbyterians, struggling in the Bay Area and living in tension nationally with their Confession of 1967, are not alone on these fields of deep strife. All the major denominations and the sects today are, in varying degrees, rife with tension, embroiled in controversy, or torn by conflict. The Lutheran Church, Missouri Synod, and the Episcopalians have sustained

[5] *Ibid.*, especially, pp. 165-92.

deep inner wounds. The Baptists' struggle to break out into the world is deep and hard. The Methodists appear to experience tension on all fronts. The United Church of Christ exhibits the head of Janus as one segment calls for secularism and the other cries out for spiritualism. The Lutheran Church in America fell flat on its face in aiming at a modest six million dollar appeal (ACT) for the urban-racial crisis. The Roman Catholic Church is torn by internal conflict over dogma, liturgy, and social ethics. The Dutch and Latin American prelates, currently strong for "the church in the world," are a challenge to the Roman traditionalists and to many Protestants too.

Most churchmen deplore these tensions and conflicts. Others rejoice in them as signs of vital Christianity. Sweeping reforms are called for if the contemporary church is to exercise Christ's ministry of reconciliation through conflict. That is the theme of the next chapter. It should be read in the context of "biblical conflict" sketched in this chapter and in the context of Christ and culture outlined in chapter 4.

*Wild, wild wind, wilt thou never cease thy sighing?*
*Dark, dark night, wilt thou never wear away?*
*Cold, cold church, in thy death sleep lying,*
*The Lent is past, thy Passion here, but not thine Easter Day.*

*Peace, faint heart, though the night be dark and sighing,*
*Rest, fair corpse, where thy Lord himself hath lain.*
*Weep, dear Lord, above thy bride low lying;*
*Thy tears shall wake her frozen limbs to life and health again.*

—Charles Kingsley

# VII

# CAN THE CHURCH HELP MAN TO BE HUMAN?

A substantial corps of critics answer that question negatively. Others simply ignore it and go about their work. Both groups are convinced that the institutional church, like Custer at Little Big Horn, has made its last stand. The only unfinished task, as they see it, belongs to the burial detail. It is their judgment that the institutional church, "precious in its own sight," is "renewingly unrenewed." [1] They are convinced that renewal was an activity which the institutional church

[1] Among the current critiques, Robert S. Lecky's and H. Elliott Wright's *Can These Bones Live?* (New York: Sheed & Ward, 1969) is rousing and journalistic.

employed unsuccessfully in the 1960's for its own survival. Their conclusion is firm—the organized church is irrelevant to man-come-of-age.[2]

But the vigorous stirrings in Catholic, Protestant, and Orthodox circles during the last two decades undermine this sweeping appraisal. These stirrings have been widespread enough to cause renewers to hope, traditionalists to dig in, and reactionaries to launch mean-spirited attacks. Presently, the lines between the renewalists and the traditionalists in the American church are being sharply drawn.[3] The forces appear to be evenly matched; but the balance of power would shift to the status quoers if the reactionaries join them. The basic question then is: Can the institutional church come to grips with itself in a modern, technological, secular society? Specifically, can the churches of white, middle America manage responsible involvement with blacks, poor whites, young people, senior citizens, and dissenters of all ages? Can an Americanized Protestant-Catholic-Orthodox church understand and accept Asiatics, Africans, and Latin Americans who reject violently their arrogant North Atlantic community? Can church members accept the inherent anguish in gospel faith which alienates as well as unites?

If the institutional church is to help man to become human, it must identify, evaluate, and wrestle with interlocking theological, social, economic, and political aspects of human life. It must prune its dead traditions. It must interpret its vital traditions relevantly. The institutional church—preoccupied narcissistically

[2] Jacques Ellul has severe doubts about the renewal of his Reformed Church in France, the relevance of the World Council of Churches, and the efficacy of political action. Cf. his "Mirror of These Ten Years," *The Christian Century*, February 18, 1970, pp. 200-204.

[3] See Jeffrey Hadden, *The Gathering Storm in the Churches* (New York: Harper & Row, 1969).

with its internal condition while venturing peripatetically into the world—has moved from the church page to the front page of the local newspaper. But it continues to be tardy in getting where the action is. It continues to be the taillight. Even where church members do accept the biblical mandate to serve Christ in the world, ecclesiastical structures are too cumbersome and too rigid for effective social involvement. Another complicating factor is that the grass-roots church is reluctant to anticipate the implications of social change so that it can prepare itself to serve persons where they are. Its professional leadership has been cautions. Prognostication is not compatible with an institution which, since the tenth century, has been the most reluctant among the social institutions to adapt to change and to break new frontiers. Except for the sixteenth century in Western Europe, the eighteenth century in England, and the stirrings today, the worldly (human) character of the gospel appears to be locked away in the first several centuries of Christian history. The institutional church is tradition-oriented rather than venture-oriented.

Obviously, prognostication is risky in any field. Several weeks after the stock market crash in 1929, a distinguished professor of economics at Yale University predicted confidently that this nation's economic life would surge forward within a few months! His erroneous prediction led one hard-pressed businessman to quip in 1930: "If all the economists were laid end to end, they would not reach a conclusion." Social predictions are dangerous because events tend to outrun the estimates of the ablest social analysts. Kenneth Galbraith, discussing in later 1969 his significant book, *The Affluent Society* (published, 1959), stated flatly that if he had predicted the racial revolution when he wrote that book he would have been charged with insanity. Further, he admitted that he had no notion in 1959 that racial revolution would sweep America in the 1960's.[4] Man is not privy to God's ways. Accurate prognosis, like the full understanding of anything, is beyond any human mind until movements have reached their completion. God's thoughts always outstrip man's thoughts. From Gamaliel to Paul VI, institutional churchmen have wanted "to be sure," and in effect that is atheism. Either the church, accepting "the rainbow sign," risks its institutional life or it negates God's grace. And risks are inherent in every prediction and experiment.

It was relatively easy for space specialists, given the scientific data, to predict accurately the moon landings. It is impossible for the State Department, the CIA, or cloistered political scientists to predict accurately what a particular segment of human beings in the Middle East will do next week. To estimate and project the impact of the future on our social institutions and to plan flexibly for those expected changes is hazardous; but it is essential. The church, like other social institutions, has the choice of total unpreparedness and increasing irrelevance or rational planning and intelligent experimentation if it intends to help man to be human in tomorrow's world.[5]

The church—culturally accommodationist in the 40's, preoccupied with institutional aggrandizement in the 50's, earnestly liberal in the 60's, and increasingly reactionary in the early 70's—must come to terms with the Spirit of God who, brooding over the world, is sowing seeds of new life and opening wide doors on

[4] *The Atlantic*, May, 1969.

[5] Lyle Schaller, *The Impact of the Future* (Nashville: Abingdon, 1969), focuses helpfully on this cultural limitation.

his world. Otherwise, God's humanization of man will go on apart from the church's co-partnership with him. The institutional church as we know it will become a relic. If the church is to follow the Pioneer of Life into the world, churchmen must effect radical changes in the centers of theological education, the local ministries (parish, academic, specialized), ecumenical relationships at the grass roots, ecclesiastical structures, and their attitude toward God's world.

No one can predict which of the current trends in contemporary theology will become dominant during the 70's or whether a radically new theology will surface. But two concerns are likely to be dominant in the theology of the 70's: the reality of God and the possibility of realizing a humane community in an urban-technocratic society. The God is dead theology, the secular city theology, situation ethics, the theology of hope, *et al.*, have had an impact on *the world in the church.* But as John Macquarrie, Oxford University, points out, the church has not examined fully the deep implications of these new theologies and thrusts in social ethics. It has raced from one to another of them without digesting any. But at least these theologies and social thrusts have convinced responsible churchmen that any theology must address basic human concerns in the language of contemporary man. It cannot exist as the academic possession of a few. Like political science and economics, theology must speak to people where they are.

It was needful to call the twentieth-century church to sacrificial involvement in the world; it always will be. It was needful to remind the contemporary church that it exists to serve God and man here and now; it always will be. But if the contemporary church is to be transformed from little bands of commandos into a disciplined army; if it wants to move beyond peripatetic experimentation; if it aims to break free of "renewal activities" designed to serve institutional needs, a substantial corps of laity must be motivated to wrestle with doctrinal and ethical questions in the context of the gospel *and* social change. The need for serious "God-talk" (the Anglo Saxon equivalent for theology) is crucial in all human situations. The church should initiate and carry on these dialogues. But it is ill equipped to do so. It is sketchy about the Faith, parochial in its understanding of other world views, and naïve about the uses of political power in the world. Denis de Rougemont argues cogently that today's earnest Christian finds himself in a situation which is utterly insane: a world where the faith "is denied, more or less serenely ignored, or, even worse, where Christianity is accepted and ridiculed under the form of its traditional deviations, its caricatures; in short, in a world where it does not exist." [6]

In too many quarters church members are disenchanted with the institution, biblically illiterate, theologically naïve. They need to be motivated to study the scriptures and equipped to employ their witness to truth as a frame of reference for forging personal and societal relationships. The laity's outspoken criticisms or quiet rejection of the church's teachings (content, language, logic) must be heard and considered, challenged and affirmed. Laymen who think for themselves will not accept irrelevant dogmas. They will not respond to shallow homilies on "religion." They will not get involved in the community of faith through evangelistic programs designed to "con" newcomers into joining the local congregation. The popular response to studies

[6] *The Christian Opportunity* (New York: Holt, Rinehart & Winston, 1963), p. 10.

like *Honest to God, The Secular City, Situation Ethics, Theology of Hope,* and writings on Vatican II demonstrate that a substantial segment of the laity are able and willing to examine social issues in the light of Christian doctrine and ethics.

Equally significant is the fact that many people outside the church—confused by the tempo of social change; at odds with a traditional view of war as part of diplomacy between sovereign states; increasingly sensitive to the dehumanizing forces inherent in poverty, institutional bureaucracy, and status society; and searching for authentic values in an age of relativism—are wrestling with issues which are eschatological as well as mundane. In fact, Paul Goodman contends that alienated persons in our society are asking theological questions more earnestly than most church members are asking them. Many worldly people are eager for theological dialogue if the conversations are set in the context of concerned action and "languaged" to communicate reality. But that dialogue will be stillborn unless churchmen are motivated, equipped, and encouraged to carry their end of it.

But the blind cannot lead the blind. On the whole, the church's schools of theology have not turned out "professionals" who have been notably effective in motivating and equipping the laity for effective Christian ministry.

## *CONCERNING THEOLOGICAL EDUCATION*

A. It is crucial that the theological centers of education bring the Old and New Testaments together in the learning experience of the student. God's progressive self-revelation culminating in the historical Person of his son provides the scriptures' primary unity and points up their personal and social relevance. But this essential unity and relevance, endorsed in theory in most theological schools, is in fact shattered or obscured in many. As Caesar divided Gaul into three parts, contemporary theological education (not fundamentalist) has effected its own three partitions: the Old Testament, a course requirement to be suffered; the New Testament, a source book of sermonic texts and social action slogans; revelation, a "thing" to be possessed or ignored. The theological centers of education have not produced clergy who have been able to equip laymen to discern the Word of God in the words of men (biblical revelation), and to join God at work in contemporary history (ongoing revelation). Consequently, God's authority is ignored in the American parish; each member is a law unto himself; the local congregation is primarily a social unit. The one-Lord-one baptism-one-faith principle is rarely operative in the grass-roots church. Understandably, the world is neither attracted to nor repelled by its message; it is simply indifferent.

Clergy and laity alike think of the New Testament as "the scriptures." It is not that and never has been by itself. Gustav Wingren has pointed out that the isolation of the New Testament as "the scriptures" is a modern phenomenon unknown to the Reformation and Catholic Orthodoxy. It is the Old Testament that is called "scripture" in the New Testament, and it is esential to establishing Jesus' humanity.[7] The New Testament is not the Bible; the Old Testament is not the Bible. As a whole they constitute the biblical witness to God's progressive self-revelation inside history. Theological students should be trained in the sciences which deal with the texts and meanings of the Old and New Testaments,

[7] Gustav Wingren, *Gospel and Church* (Philadelphia: Fortress Press, 1964), pp. 30-31, 48-49, 69, 84, 99-100.

but this necessary task must be accomplished without fragmenting the biblical revelation. When the New Testament, ripped from historical context, becomes the church's Bible, a "Jesus cult" emerges, and cultic religion is not morally relevant to man's situation.

Biblical theology is always relevant to man-in-society. When, for example, the laity are brought to the realization that Pharaoh's pursuit of the Israelites was not included in scripture to provide a chase scene for a Cecil B. DeMille movie but because God had shattered the economic structure of Egypt which rested on conscripted labor, they have an historical perspective for recognizing that God is concerned about social and economic justice for persons in their society. John 3:16, stripped of churchly sentiment and read in the context of Amos' searing judgment on a society which treated widows and orphans as things, enables twentieth-century churchmen to recognize that the God they worship calls them, as he did Amos, to challenge discriminatory housing, inequitable employment practices, and separate education in their communities now. Conversion and responsible social action go hand in hand in authentic Christian experience. If a man says he loves God but does not also love his fellow men, he is a liar. Standing in the prophetic tradition, Jesus made that bald estimate. It is biblical to contend that the personal and the social gospel are inseparable.

*B.* A wide gulf is fixed between the theoretical and practical learning experience of theological students. Efforts to bridge this chasm have been underway for several decades: field work, clinical training in counseling, participation in experimental ministries, etc. But these efforts to bridge the gulf between the academic and the practical must be speeded up at once. Too many seminary graduates are not prepared to deal with the ambiguities inherent in congregational life and communities. The polarization in some congregations today roots partially in their seminary education. There have been significant breakthroughs in a few schools (notably Toronto and Cleveland), but most theological schools have only flirted with the idea of combining the theoretical and the practical in the student's learning experience. Unless the chasmic gulf is eliminated during the 70's, the rising ineffectiveness of the clergy in the field could fracture the local ministries through mounting irrelevance, frustration, and hostility. It will also alienate able men from considering a vocation in the church.

Bridging the chasm will require the recruitment of competent men from the local ministries to team-teach, provide electives, and conduct seminars. Parish pastors and theological professors alike will benefit from these give-and-take exchanges in interdisciplinary teaching (rarely tried), but it will be the students who will benefit most. Presently, the church lags far behind business and industry, the medical sciences, and the psychological sciences in bringing theoreticians and practitioners together in theological learning experiences. In the church, the dichotomy between the two disciplines must be eliminated promptly. It is five minutes to twelve on the cloistered seminary's Cinderella clock. The time for thorough-going reform was immediately after World War I.

C. Theological education must also develop interdisciplinary teaching in cooperation with secular education. This will necessitate proximity to and active relations with a secular university. The only alternative is the full-time employment of secular professors qualified to teach history, sociology, psychology, and political science in our prestigious secular institutions.

This is neither practical nor expedient. Decades ago, H. Richard Niebuhr observed that "theological inquiry is not something that can be added to humanistic and naturalistic studies; it needs to be constantly informed by them and to inform them." Professional churchmen agreed, yet went on doing what comes naturally to most denominational churchmen—preserving dear old alma mater. Locating a seminary adjacent to a secular university in an urban center will not automatically place its faculty and students in dialogue with intellectuals, humanists, and hard-nosed materialists but it will provide opportunities for those theologians and students who want to be informed by and to inform humanistic, naturalistic, and materialistic studies.

Another aspect of interdisciplinary teaching and learning requires the clustering of denominational and Catholic centers of theological education. The 1966 *Report of the American Association of Theological Schools* documented that a rigid denominational and parochial outlook continues to characterize the majority of theological schools. The cluster concept presents multiple problems, but the potential opportunities make the risk legitimate.[8] Wherever theological schools cluster with a brace of denominational seminaries and a Catholic seminary (or two), and the cluster works at relating to a secular university and the university is hospitable to them, a servant church may emerge in our broken, bleeding society. As Germany cornered Belgium into heroism in 1914, the church may be cornered into serving people at the grass roots by the escalating demands imposed on it by a radically changing society.[9]

[8] *Moving into the Future,* A Report on Developing Cooperation Among Seminaries, AATS, 534 Third National Building, Dayton, Ohio.

[9] King Leopold described Belgium's stand in 1914 in this fashion.

It would be a mistake to assume that the clustering of seminaries will alone provide the panacea for the ills that beset theological education. Indeed, we have to recognize in all candor that clustering is no way to provide validation for the continued existence of a seminary that really ought to go out of business, and denominational executives still must face the question of how many seminaries their churches can legitimately support. It is also clear that some of the most innovative programs of education for ministry are found in schools that are still relatively unrelated to others. Especially in the early stages, the complexities of clustering often divert energy and attention away from pressing needs for educational reform.

The evidence that is already in, however, indicates that with admitted exceptions clustering can provide the basis on which serious reform must be built. While it is possible to be attracted by potential financial savings, sober planners are well aware that this can be illusory and that the only overarching goal that can be sought is the pursuit of excellence in preparing men for ministry. The experience to date continues to support the conviction of the Resources Planning Commission that the development of cooperative programs that clusters make possible is a massive step forward in the achievement of that goal.[10]

The widespread notion in denominational circles that these and other considerations on theological education are beyond the understanding of laymen is nonsense. Should hospital boards be peopled only with doctors or juries with lawyers? Laymen who are able to comprehend complex intellectual problems in other realms and who are experienced in fashioning and administering corporations should be invited (on a six-to-one laymen-clerical ratio) into the decision-making councils on theological education. As Karl Rahner has

[10] *Moving into the Future,* AATS Report.

pointed out, "The knowledge and experience of the living God is not a privilege of the clergy." [11]

## *THE LOCAL MINISTRIES*

Next, we want to identify several basic changes which must be effected in the local ministries if the institutional church is to help man to be human.

A. It is imperative in every local situation that the clerical and lay leaders distinguish between strategy and tactics. Biblically viewed, there is only one strategy. The community of faith is called out of the world to share the Living Word (Christ) in the world through persons with other persons, any one of whom is free to ignore, reject, or attack the Word and its bearer, or to accept God's authority in his life. Any tactic which implements this basic strategy in any place at any time is acceptable to God and helpful to man and society. The theological and psycho-social implications of this strategy point up the need for laity and clergy to re-examine the reality of God, the meaning of revelation, the implications of human freedom, the nature of faith, and the need for personal and social discipline.

B. There is crucial need for radical renewal in the local ministries where laity and clergy treat one another as objects rather than as persons called by God to serve persons. Some concrete questions must be answered specifically in parish after parish. Do the lay leaders regard their clergy as bold spokesmen for God or as managers paid to serve the local corporation? Does the official board view its staff as hired hands to be "had" at the lowest salaries possible? In congregations which believe that "the laborer deserves his wages,"

[11] Quoted by Thomas Franklin O'Meara, O.P., "Is There a Common Authority for Christians?" *The Ecumenical Review* XXII (January, 1970), 26.

the official board provides an adequate staff, reviews their competence periodically, remunerates them accordingly, and provides for their growth in professional competence. Where that is not possible—and it is not in economically deprived areas, mission congregations, and experimental ministries—the denomination or cooperative church bodies will subsidize these local ministries responsibly or decline to initiate them. Secular man disdains a church which provides sanctuary for incompetent professionals. Secular man also recoils from a church which expects competent lay and clerical workers to endure economic hardship in an affluent society. In many places, the church adheres to a business ethic which is inferior to that practiced in the business community, yet carps hypocritically at the competitive economic society. The truth is that many able clergy, like creative teachers, are shamefully underpaid. In an affluent society this means essentially that they are undervalued. It is this undervaluation which causes many able teachers and clergy to lose heart and deters others from taking up either profession.

But if the laity view their clergy as objects to be manipulated, exploited, and tolerated, it is equally true that the clergy look on the laity as objects, too. Some pastors lament the limitations of their parishioners instead of accepting, challenging, instructing, and shepherding them into a vital relationship with Christ and leading their congregations into cooperative ministries concerned to build a more humane society under God. The lawyer does not complain that his client is in trouble with the law. The accountant does not complain that his client's records are a mess. The medical doctor does not complain that his patient is ill. But many clergy do complain that their laymen are recalcitrant, uneducated, parochial, ungenerous, etc. Church administrators (bishops and synodical and conference presidents), instead of confronting and counseling, are inclined to sympathize superficially with these men and shuffle them into other parishes where they continue to respond neurotically to strong-minded (and often equally neurotic) laymen. Pastoral care lags. The growing practice of counseling these clergy and providing them with opportunities to increase their professional competence is one clear evidence of authentic renewal in the institutional church.

On the other hand, some clergy get so involved in trying to change social structures (a necessary task) that they escape the arduous task of equipping and nurturing the church members for service in the world (the church's essential task). It is less demanding for some clergy to join protest marches than it is to prepare biblically grounded, socially relevant sermons which *persuade* church members to make their witness in the world. It is less demanding for some clergy to speak at peace rallies than it is for them to counsel sanely, face-to-face, with generous church members who honestly think that campus disturbances are Communist inspired. Mature Christians engage in both tasks. Either without the other (essentially speaking) is a fractured ministry.

Of course, there are still too many clergy who expand church facilities at the expense of the congregation's servant role in the community or scheme to keep doors open in "churches" which are in reality social enclaves or cultic societies. Parish pastors, seminary professors, and church executives must face up to a deep-rooted ecclesiastical schizophrenia which separates preaching from pastoral ministry, teaching from pastoral counseling, social action from biblical witness, and the efficient administration of an institution from the pastoral care of persons. Until the clergy see themselves as *persons* called and ordained to help persons meet Christ in the scriptures, worship, the sacraments, preaching, and the world; and as persons called to equip laymen to render priestly service to their fellow men and to fashion social institutions which are hospitable to humanity, Christ cannot humanize man through the institutional church.

C. Each local ministry must step up the tempo in establishing working relationships with other ministries across denominational lines. Local councils of churches which foster and undergird interdenominational cluster ministries in urban and metropolitan areas are effective instruments. Where there is openness and candor, Protestant, Catholic, and Orthodox ministries will fashion cooperative ventures to serve God and man. At the same time these will cooperate eagerly with Jewish and secular agencies in concrete ventures designed to produce a more humane society. Wherever local ministries seek seriously to serve God and man they will give up their "solo" witness and/or denominational exclusiveness, listen attentively to other accents on the gospel, examine critically the secular styles of witness (Peace Corps, Vista, etc.), and link forces with any group which endeavors to enable persons to become more human. The dangers in this unprecedented flexibility are obvious, but the possible gains force such risks in faith. Wherever people find common answers to pressing social problems they will also find a deeper sense of community.[12] If, however, cooperative ventures are undertaken simply to prolong the life of ineffective local ministries (or because the clergy consider it an "in" thing), God will not prosper those ventures. The

[12] Jürgen Moltmann, "Politics and the Practice of Hope," *The Christian Century*, March 11, 1970, pp. 288-301.

renewal of man and society is not an activity designed for the church's institutional survival or aggrandizement.

*D.* Many congregations across America pay their denominational apportionment regularly, find their pews comfortably filled Sunday after Sunday, provide well-staffed church schools, accept and orient to evangelistic and stewardship practices which reflect biblical goals, are housed in adequate buildings, and are socially involved. Some of these ministries benefit from hospitable geographical-cultural situations. That is not a crime; affluent people need to become human, too. Others, in less hospitable situations, owe their vitality to imaginative clerical and lay leadership. These should be studied closely for clues to renewal. All reflect a measure of commitment, courage, and compassion. But these Christian attributes characterize thousands of local ministries which are not prospering. The stronger ministries—alert to insidious pride, flat complacency, and cruel indifference—will accept God's call to initiate creative relationships with well-motivated but hard-pressed ministries in their own and other denominations. Regional churchmanship is a "must." Further, "successful" ministries will inquire daily of their Lord: "Is our strength in the gospel or . . . ?"

*E.* Finally, a majority of the local ministries need to reevaluate preaching as an effective function of ministry.

The gospels testify that Jesus beamed his teaching at twelve men. He worked steadily with small groups. The Christian church had its beginning in an upper room, with two men on the Emmaus Road, in the home of Priscilla and Aquilla, in the catacombs, and in hundreds of other places where handfuls of people gathered surreptitiously in Christ's name. During the first three centuries of its life, the church, prevented by

Roman law from assembling publicly, did not experience heavily attended public services. Mass rallies and cathedral churches were undreamed of.

Authentic learning experiences in church, university, business, government, and family do require dialogue, encounter, confrontation, conflict, and reconciliation. Luther's "table talks," Wesley's class meetings, the Sons of Liberty (1765–1775), the nineteenth-century Abolitionists, James' classes at Harvard—random examples—are historical evidences that people are enlightened and motivated in small groups. Elton Trueblood, John Casteel, and Reuel Howe have been pressing this claim for years. It is consonant with traditional Christianity.

But the church, after Constantine legalized Christianity, has also proclaimed the gospel and taught evangelically in large assemblies. Luther and Wesley, effective catalysts in group discussions, preached regularly to large public gatherings. Chrysostom, Peter the Hermit, Francis of Assisi, Savonarola, Whitefield, Moody, and Graham preached effectively to throngs of people. On any Sunday this year, several hundred thousand clergymen will "preach" to seventy million Americans in church. That is also a strand in traditional Christianity. Jesus addressed immense crowds. Centuries later the preceptive Kierkegaard observed: "The Word of God divides a crowd into individuals." Paul Althaus, a German theologian who died recently, insisted that modern man is not tired of preaching; he is tired of our preaching!

It will be apostasy if the church—stubbornly rooted in Western Europe, institutionally vigorous in North America, and showing signs of vigorous life in Africa, South America, and Asia—relegates preaching to a minor place during the decade of the 70's. The power of the spoken word has been and continues to be a significant force in the turbulent history of the twentieth century. It has persuaded individuals in large assemblies to precise points of view, specific attitudes, and concrete deeds. John Kennedy captured the imagination of millions with his inaugural address, his "Ich bin ein Berliner" speech, and his somber TV address at the time of the 1962 nuclear confrontation. Martin Luther King, Jr., a preacher to the end, persuaded millions of blacks and whites to get involved in the civil rights movement. Garrison, Beecher, Parker, and thousands of other preachers fostered the abolitionist movement in the nineteenth century. During the violent twentieth century, Hitler, Roosevelt, Churchill, Robert Kennedy, George Wallace, the Beatles, Arlo Guthrie, Joan Baez, Mario Savio, and Mark Rudd spoke or sang persuasively to huge assemblies of people. As in Jesus' day, the children of this generation are wiser than the children of light!

Zealous advocates of the small group movement appear to be oblivious to the implications of these secular realities for the church. Properly concerned to recover a neglected strand in teaching and motivating people, they regard dialogue as a substantive solution rather than as a necessary corrective. The issue is not either/or, it is both/and. It always has been. Effective preaching and teaching in large assemblies challenges, enlightens, and motivates persons to dialogue with one another in the church and in the world. Dialogue in small groups informs, enriches, shapes, and focuses the preaching-teaching ministry in the local church, and in turn enriches it.

Theological professors and parish pastors carry the primary responsibility for prophetic-pastoral preaching in and by the church (as medical schools and medical doctors bear primary responsibility for public health).

But as an enlightened populace is also responsible for community health, so too are laymen in the church responsible for the church's preaching ministry. Until they exercise the ministry of proclamation in everyday affairs, preaching will fall short of its full effectiveness. In congregations where the professional preaching ministry is perfunctory or subservient to the social status quo or preoccupied with social action, laymen must challenge that preaching, initiate dialogue with their clergy, discuss biblical dogmas and current issues for addressment from the pulpit, and free the clergy from mundane tasks so that they can study and work to be truly professional in proclaiming Christ.

## *SOME UNANSWERED QUESTIONS*

Finally, we want to underscore again several secular issues which confront not only the church's seminaries, local ministries, and administrators, but the whole of America's citizenry. These and other pressing socio-economic-political issues are disrupting contemporary society. No single institution has brought creative solutions to bear on any one of them; no single institution can. Pat answers from traditions, however venerable, and political rhetoric only serve to deepen the social crisis. Society's hope lies in critical, cooperative, flexible, rooted, pluralistic addressments to and experimental engagements with these crucial issues. Since the stock answers hurt the social situation more than they help it, and since the church must discover how to work with other social institutions without losing its unique identity,[13] we shall recall several particularly pressing questions. Of course, complex questions do irritate people!

A. Church-state relations. This centuries-old issue is

[13] Langdon Gilkey, *How the Church Can Minister to the World Without Losing Itself* (New York: Harper & Row, 1964).

crucial in a technological-industrial-military society. Yesteryear's dogmas are meaningless in a nuclear era. Traditional approaches to war and peace are as antiquated today as Whitney's cotton gin or Watt's steam engine. In an era of established "power" nations, emerging nations, and once powerful nations in decline, Vietnam and the Middle East point up especially the irrelevance of the dogma of "the just war." This dogma had its origins in antiquity. A half dozen national denominations endorsed a variant on "the just war" when they endorsed the principle of selective conscientious objection. But that does not begin to scratch the surface of the moral question of war and peace in a nuclear age. A radical reconsideration of this complex issue is urgently needed. The church should lead.

The Cross has demonstrated for twenty centuries that the use of force between states or alliances of states, between races or segments of races, between classes or segments of classes, is fratricide in the family of God. Now, the threat of nuclear annihilation pushes that truth to the fore so forcibly that the ancient concept of "the just war" is meaningless today. A galloping technology has allowed mankind to stand in outer space with three astronauts and view this planet with electronically elongated sight. Millions of people, Christians among them, realized for the *first* time that the war in Vietnam, the clashes on the Sino-Russian border, the sniping along the 38th parallel in Korea, the violence between Arabs and Israelis, and the conflicts between whites and blacks in the United States and in South Africa are fratricide. Sovereign-national states (and sovereign power blocs) are explosive liabilities in a technological-space age. Theological schools, local ministries, church bureaucracies, and concerned citizens in general, must bring their energies and resources to bear on this dangerous social situation in imaginative ways which point to an effective outlawing of war between and among sovereign states. The church should be in the forefront of this crusade.

But what can a church in bondage to a material way of looking at life say honestly to the military-industrial state in America and Russia (and in other places a decade hence) when the dollars it employs come from an economy which is dependent on war, exploitation, and discrimination? Is the church less involved in this than the prestigious universities? What degree of disengagement is likely, or possible? Specifically, what could the church say honorably about the ABM missile system? How can churchmen judge society when they are themselves part of the problem rather than part of the answer? Can the blind lead the blind? Renewal begins in the church.

*B.* How will the church meet this generation of rebellious youth? Will it react against those who flaunt the morality of the generation which gave them life, reared them in affluence, and provided them opportunity for superior education—while requiring them to accept the current social system without critical comment, bow before the Establishment's venerated authorities, and die in the jungles of Vietnam? Will the church—eschewing simplistic, patronizing, and jaundiced judgments on young people en masse—stand eyeball to eyeball with the fractional minority who are bent on the dissolution of social institutions; will it challenge imaginatively those young people who are preparing uncritically (often cynically) to join the Establishment because they, like their elders, value comfort above character and prefer convenience to conscience; and will it "listen with affection" to the thirty percent of youth who, criticizing education, government, church, and family, are asking for a reordering of our cultural priorities? Will churchmen stone the youthful prophets who are calling both generations to candor, compassion, and commitment? Will they patronize them because young people are not aware of the ambiguities of human history? Will churchmen face the hard truth that they have accepted these ambiguities too readily? Renewal begins in the church.

C. How can the church, racist in its white constituency and increasingly race conscious in its black constituency, respond creatively to the inhumanities which racism, poverty, affluence, and technology inflict on millions of human beings? Will the church (black and white) seek to understand the anguish of those who, like Eldridge Cleaver, proclaim violently: "We shall have our manhood. We shall have it or the earth will be levelled by our attempts to gain it."[14] Can a class-oriented white church face reality and rise penitently and hopefully to meet the needs of the economically poor in the urban ghettos, Appalachia, the Indian reservations, the vineyards of California, and the poor in spirit in the ghettos of suburbia? Will the American church, rejecting the house religion of Nixonia, take up the prophet's mantle and expose those national and local political leaders who consciously and unconsciously manipulate people and exploit social conflict to strengthen their party, and will they support those political leaders who work primarily to direct the vast resources of our government into humane ventures? Will the American church help to persuade the prosperous American state to employ its unprecedented technological means and unparalleled economic re-

[14] Eldridge Cleaver, *Soul on Ice* (New York: McGraw-Hill, 1968), p. 61.

sources to make the world more hospitable to human beings, seventy percent of whom are poverty ridden.[15] Will the grass-roots church get involved with complex human needs and ecological demands in each locality and live firsthand with tension and conflict? Renewal begins in the church.

*D.* In an era of deepening alienation between and among nations, classes, and races; in families and among institutions, will the church claim God's grace, accept his demands, and become a reconciling fellowship for bruised, bleeding, broken persons? Renewal begins in the church.

Faced with these and other crushing issues, so many churchmen simply throw up their hands in despair: the task is too large, the resources are too limited, the time is too short. "What will be, will be." Others continue to plod along serving the institutional aims of a bureaucratic church without inquiring whether it serves God's purpose in humanizing man. But here and there, some are stirred daily by Christ and the evident needs of humanity to take heart and try again, to be concerned for persons, to endure hardship, to hope in God's tomorrow. And into the hands of this new community of persons God entrusts the future of the world he loves.

Renewal then is always social, but it is never wholly social. It begins in individuals who, accepting Christ's authority, become part of his new community and work privately and publicly to bring their "given" society into the world. Man in process of renewal and his halting efforts to reorder society along humane lines

[15] The popular notion that the United States government is doing more for underdeveloped countries than any other nation is erroneous. Only .03% of the GNP gets into this kind of aid. The richest nation in the world ranks tenth (proportionately) on foreign aid. Russia outstrips us. By 1975 France will be providing 1% of its GNP for foreign aid.

breed tension, stir controversy, and engender conflict. The church must accept this in the confidence that God will effect reconciliation through elemental conflicts which are engendered for the sake of humanity.

The Cross was the price Jesus paid for the humanization of man and society. The servant is not above his Master.